WRITE COMPELLING FICTION

SUCCESSFUL INDIE AUTHOR: BOOK 4

L.J. MARTIN

CRAIG MARTELLE

Write Compelling Fiction
(or any other type of writing)

Successful Indie Author, Book 4

by

L.J. Martin & Craig Martelle

Successful Indie Author - a series for self-published authors

Successful Indie Author, Book 1 - Become a Successful Indie Author - https://geni.us/BecomeSuccessful

Successful Indie Author, Book 2 - Release Strategies - https://geni.us/ReleaseStrategies

Successful Indie Author, Book 3 - Collaborations - https://geni.us/Collaborations

Write Compelling Fiction

Wolfpack Publishing
6032 Wheat Penny Avenue
Las Vegas, NV 89122

wolfpackpublishing.com

Editing services provided by Lynne Stiegler
Cover by Sapphire Designs
Formatting (both eBook and paperback) by Drew Avera

This is a book on writing books. If that wasn't your desire in buying this eBook, then please return it within seven days for a full refund from Amazon.

eBook ISBN 978-1-64119-845-5
Paperback ISBN 978-1-64119-846-2

Library of Congress Control Number: 2019948576

TABLE OF CONTENTS

NOTE FROM LARRY

As it has several times during the thirty years my wife and I have been involved in the publishing business, once again the business itself has made a radical change. And, as always, when things change in a momentous way, those involved have mixed emotions. The evolution of ebooks and reading on digital devices like phones or tablets, and the ease of publishing those ebooks, is not only an evolution but a revolution.

Now anyone can be published and what I wrote in this book a few years ago, as far as getting published, is a totally different subject and has been rewritten so the aspiring writer can find him- or herself with a published book in hand, either in paper or on an ebook reader. However, success, if judged by actual book sales, is another matter altogether.

What hasn't changed is how to write a compelling novel. That's a constant.

This book is dedicated to all those thousands, or maybe millions, who've submitted a novel and had it rejected, then placed it on a garage or closet shelf, where it languished forever —and it was perhaps the best novel of the year. Or could have been, with very little additional work.

And to the thick-skinned who kept submitting, submitting, submitting!

And to those who decided to self-publish via that fantastic new resource, the internet. Amazon, Smashwords, Nook and many other bookselling websites have opened a whole new world to those not only willing to write, but to work at selling their writing. And to those who've tied up with ebook publishers, such as our own Wolfpack Publishing LLC, which is cutting a wide swath in ebook marketing.

Now, onto the meat of things.

Never underestimate the power of fiction.

Prolific author Sir Walter Scott singlehandedly ruined the opal market. Opals were as valuable as diamonds or rubies—until Scott wrote about an enchanted opal that caused the death of a fictional heroine. The price of opals dropped by half!

I wrote this volume some eleven years ago, updated once in between, still forever long ago in internet years, and then partnered with science fiction author Craig Martelle to bring this to the next generation of writers through his work with over 32,000 indies via Michael Anderle's 20Booksto50k® self-published author group. Craig has four books with a traditional publishing house and over 100 that are self-published. He brings a great deal of knowledge regarding the current state of the digital market and how that relates to those authors who are able to manage the complete production and publication process themselves. Authors are small businesses, with all the challenges that come with a logistic train and government regulations along with distributor foibles. Craig has navigated these waters well and is a perennial top 100 Science Fiction author on Amazon, where he leverages their distribution horsepower to his benefit.

See more on L. J. Martin, and his wife, Kat Martin, NYT bestselling romantic suspense author on the Websites below:

www.ljmartin.com

www.katbooks.com

NOTE FROM CRAIG

Mike Bray from Wolfpack asked me to talk with Larry about a book on writing fiction. I downloaded Larry's book immediately and read it. There were gems peppered throughout, those things that a good author subconsciously considers. The rest of us have to write with intentionality, reviewing with an editor's eye while still telling the story. There was also an opportunity to update the book with the self-publishing speed of the modern internet. An author's world has been transformed by ease of access and the ability to conduct in-depth research without ever leaving the comfort of one's home. It is the new way of doing business. The roles remain the same regarding author, agent, traditional publishing house, acquisition editor, and publisher, but not in the same way. With the mastery of self-publishing, an author can skip the steps regarding an agent and going through an acquisition editor to get a traditional publishing contract. The author also reaps the reward of not having to share profits. The required quality of storytelling remains the same as the readers are discerning and the final arbiter of whether a book is good or not. That's what we're going to focus on in this book.

See more on Craig Martelle, International Bestselling Author on the Website below:

https://craigmartelle.com

OTHER BOOKS IN THIS SERIES:

Successful Indie Author Book 1: Become a Successful Indie Author
https://geni.us/BecomeSuccessful

Successful Indie Author Book 2: Release Strategies
https://geni.us/ReleaseStrategies

Successful Indie Author Book 3: Collaborations
https://geni.us/Collaborations

INTRODUCTION

This book is written for those who, like me, are neither English majors nor grammarians—although even those of you who are may glean some good common sense and novelists' tricks from it. The devil of the craft of writing fiction is that being an English major has little to do with it.

Grammar is important, but "I couldn't put it down" is a compliment not gleaned because of perfect grammar. Grammar is only one of the reasons fiction is compelling—only one of the many reasons why that most cherished of compliments comes to you as a fiction writer. Still, you don't want to put off a reader with bad grammar—you don't want to break the reader's trance.

I'm a guy who loves to hunt, fish, or carry my cameras outdoors for almost any reason. Like most of you, I've worked hard all my life. I love the West and its history, and I'd have done just fine had I lived a hundred and fifty years ago. As the song says, a country boy will survive. But it would be hard to survive without a good book in hand—a book that elicits the writer's favorite compliment: "I couldn't put it down."

I do love a good novel or a beautifully crafted work of nonfiction.

But to be published (conventionally with legacy publishers or self-published), you need more than a love of reading. Be it driving an eighteen wheeler, driving a nail, or doing nails, there are skills to be learned in any profession. For a writer, there are skills to be learned, and there are also tricks that make writing a novel easier to accomplish and much easier to sell. You need to have a compelling story that will cause readers to tell others about your book, or will drive readers to buy your next or other books.

There are also pitfalls. Fortunately, most of them are easily avoided.

Many years ago, I wanted to write and sell a novel. I learned *how* the hard way. By studying other's mistakes (and your own) you can learn the easy way. Even today, after selling over forty book-length works and having dozens of articles published, I fight obvious mistakes, poor grammar, clumsy sentence structure, and worse—much worse—boring narrative. I can't begin to teach you all there is to know about writing novels or even writing a good letter (more likely an e-mail today). But I *can* tell you where and how to learn a good deal of it.

We're still studying, but if we can make it a little easier for you, then we've accomplished our purpose in writing this book. It's what good writers do because tomorrow's book needs to be better than yesterday's. We believe that.

Most of the rules for writing novels are valid for writing in general. A few are specific to novels, and a few are specific to genre. If you don't know the definition of *genre*, then you're exactly the person for whom this book is written. But even those of you who do know what it means will find some gems in here —most of them openly filched from much better writers than us. No, we're not above learning from others. That's what this book is all about. Don't let the lessons from westerns, historicals, or science fiction throw you off. This stuff is universal.

A great deal of what I have to say refers to thrillers (or suspense), westerns, historicals, or romance, because these, and screenplays, are what my wife and I write and how we make our living. With Craig Martelle's expertise in science fiction (some four million words published and hundreds of thousands of books sold). He has a good idea of what works. He also learned certain lessons the hard way. There's no need for you to make those same mistakes. Learn from ours. Learn from our successes, too.

We've put this book together with a main focus on westerns, but with romance, historical fiction, thrillers, and science fiction thrown in to cover most of the bases because we've found that there are universals that apply across the board, regardless of genre.

Good luck with your fiction writing—your compelling fiction—the story the reader can't put down.

"The next thing that happens in the story, is the next thing of interest that happens to the characters."

David Lean, Director

WRITE COMPELLING FICTION

1

FROM BROKER TO BOOKS?

Most of my early life was spent as a real estate broker, selling farms and ranches, subdivision land and lots. I was very, very successful at that task, but I had the urge to write. I tried a novel at the ripe old age of twenty-four and, after four chapters, found I had little to say. Later in life, unmarried and living on a boat with time on my hands, I decided if I were ever going to fulfill this smoldering ambition, now was the time.

After completing a 500-page historical novel, I submitted it a few times and got a few form rejections. It dawned on me that I had (as I have a tendency to do) plunged in where angels fear to tread. Only then did I decide to study the craft. I was lucky enough to marry a lady who approached things a little differently. She's a great study, formerly a great student, and had the background — good grounding in college-level English. And she's a voracious reader. She, too, had the urge to write. Together, we went to conferences and, separately, we wrote our own books, although we collaborated on one novel, *Tin Angel.*

After many conferences and many, many more hours in front of the word processor, the hard work began to pay off.

One of my novels, *Rush to Destiny*, was nominated as a finalist as the best biographical novel of 1992 by a group of New York reviewers and the magazine *Romantic Times /Rave Reviews*. Another, *The Benicia Belle*, was a runner-up for the Western Writers of America Spur Award for best original western paperback of 1992. It was one of over forty novels submitted that year.

Kat, my wife, (www.katmartin.com) has seen her later books repeatedly on the bestseller lists (her AGAINST series has hit the *New York Times* nine times as of this writing) and she has won many awards. She's a *New York Times* bestseller, and is internationally published in over a dozen languages and in over two dozen countries. She's earning more than she ever did in the real estate business—and she did very well in real estate!

Throughout this book I've used the masculine gender, but I have a great respect for all the wonderful, talented women who write novels—even westerns or thrillers, commonly considered "men's fiction"—or want to write them, and for the women who read them.

No matter who you are or what your age, if you can read and understand this book, you can write a novel. Some of you may take a long time to do so; some of you may whip out a masterpiece in a few months.

Like most professionals, writers have their organizations. Professional organizations can make your education happen more quickly and can make your endeavors more enjoyable. It's hard to be alone in any venture, and it helps to know you have peers with the same concerns and problems you have, and with whom you can share your successes.

Western Writers of America, Inc. sponsors an annual meeting that supports western and historical writers of both fiction and nonfiction, gives awards annually to those they judge superior in their field, and publishes a bi-monthly magazine called *The Roundup*. There are some requirements to join.

Romance Writers of America (RWA) does the same for that genre, has many more members, and offers excellent support. Those interested in romance writing should join. There are no "published" requirements. RWA has a number of local chapters with meetings and support groups that are excellent for beginning writers. They also have an annual conference.

Mystery Writers of America, International Thriller Writers, and many other groups are out there for you if you want to learn and share your wants and needs. Search for them on the Web.

Some genres pay more than others, which is a result of reader popularity. But a superlative book will win fans—if the writer can get it in the hands of enough readers.

At one time, Zane Grey outsold all of them, and the western genre still enjoys a strong, faithful following. Romance commands almost 60 percent of the mass market, but there's also huge competition.

It's hard to get a western novel reviewed in national publications, as the market is admittedly small and generally not well respected—a prejudice many of us who love the West do not share. Fortunately the elitists who display an indifferent attitude or worse to western writing, which in my opinion is the backbone of the nation's literacy, are not nearly as influential as they would like to believe. There are now very few brick-and-mortar publishers who'll even entertain a western, so the market is primarily relegated to the Web.

To illustrate what I say, I'll quote my good friend Richard S. Wheeler, a great western writer, who pointed out in a recent *The Roundup* article that the *New Columbia Encyclopedia* has admiring entries on several mystery writers (over forty) yet only one patronizing entry on Zane Grey and one on Owen Wister—no mention of Pulitzer prize winner A. B. Guthrie, Jr., or of Dorothy Johnson, Frederick Faust, Glendon Swarthout, Ernest Haycox, Walter Van Tilburg Clark, William MacLeod Raine, Henry Allen, Jack Schaefer, Louis L'Amour, or a dozen others worthy of note.

We western writers "don't get no respect."

I love westerns, but I also love thrillers, suspense, mysteries, and most nonfiction. And I love to read compelling writing of any kind. And I've written and sold in more than one genre.

To write well, I keep a number of reminders posted over my monitor, so I can't help but see them every day.

REMINDERS:

Over the top of my computer, along the edges of bookshelves just over eye-high, I have taped the following:

Filter all descriptions through point of view!

Problem, Purpose, Conflict, Goal—Active Voice!

Hear, See, Taste, Touch, and Smell!

There is no scene without conflict!

Check for As, That, Was!

Each of these, and several others, has been taped there at various times throughout my writing career. I still glance at them regularly, and they are still crucial to good writing. Other writers, I'm sure, have dozens of other reminders, but these work for me. I can't tell you how many times I've finished a work, then realized I have no taste, touch and/or smell in the work. Readers are motivated to enjoy a work in many ways, and often favor one sense over another. Appeal to all the reader's senses.

This book will, among other things, tell you why I think those reminders are so important and why, if you're a reader (and you shouldn't try being a writer if you're not), you'll never be stuck for plot or characters.

"I try to leave out the parts that readers skip."
Elmore Leonard, Novelist

2

CAN YOU DO IT

Anyone who has a basic understanding of the structure of written English or is willing to learn—and has a story to tell, or the imagination to make one up—can write and sell a novel. Many more can write a nonfiction work, particularly if it's about a skill they've mastered, be it knitting or fly fishing, or bugling for elk.

First you must want to.

Every day I enjoy writing more than the day before. It continues to come easier—and it's more financially rewarding with the advent of self-publishing.

However, my writing will never be perfect. In any of my many books—even those published by Bantam, Avon and Pinnacle—that I pick up, I see something I'd like to change.

Writing is not a science, it's a craft—an art. Two and two in writing doesn't always add up to four.

I keep learning every day. Writers learn by doing, every time they sit down and face the blank page.

When I first picked up a pencil and yellow pad, I had little knowledge of spelling or sentence structure. I found that with a little time, a dictionary, and some harsh critics (mostly Kat, my beautiful wife), contributed to the eventual sale of my first western novel. My first novel, a historical, lingered on the shelf for many years before I made a buck from it.

The chief excuse for non-achievers in all areas of endeavor is: "I just don't have the time." Horse hockey! We all waste time. We watch TV. We ride in the car and dream nonproductive dreams. You can write in your mind (and most writers do) long before putting it on paper. You can record your thoughts on your phone or use a digital voice recorder and have them automatically transcribed by the latest voice to text software. It's a whole new world. Time is no excuse.

"Whether you think you can, or you think you can't —you're right."

— Henry Ford

Write in the car, at the beach, standing on the stream bank casting for trout.

There's only one way to be a writer, and that's to write. Write two pages, maybe five-hundred words per day, and in four months you will have a 60,000 word novel.

The harder you work, the luckier you get.

It took eight years for lady luck to seek me out. By then, I'd had almost forty years to harden my head. I'd read hundreds of westerns and men's adventures and many more novels of other genres, and I thought I knew how it was done. But I didn't even know the questions yet, much less the answers. And for the first six of the eight years I wrote before I sold, I didn't bother to ask. Form rejection slips told me I wasn't doing it right. I decided it must be a craft, like painting a picture or building a fine saddle, and I decided to learn it. So I went to classes and conferences. Two years after we began that effort, Kat and I sold our first novels. Six wasted years! I should have known better as I'd been a salesman in the past, and almost quit before I decided that it, too, was a craft, and studied to learn how to sell. Then I became successful.

I'll show you how and why the question "How do you get your ideas?" is such a foolish one. History, current events, the newspaper, the television, your everyday life—all are replete with ideas for every genre, including science fiction.

Now sit back, read, then do what you've always wanted to do—write a novel.

"He's a good enough liar to write books."

From Kipling's *Captain's Courageous*

3

SELF PUBLISHING...WHAT'S IT ALL ABOUT

It's a new world in publishing now that we have companies such as Amazon, Smashwords, Apple Books, Barnes & Noble, Kobo, and many others. You are in charge of the entire process. There are steps that every author must go through.

1. Write a great story (book)
2. Edit the book
3. Put a cover on the book
4. Write the blurb for the book (back cover copy for physical books)
5. Develop a launch strategy
6. Publish the book
7. Sell the book

If your book is traditionally published, that is, with a legacy publisher, they provide the editors and covers, but the author still has a greater role than simply writing the book. If you are self-published, you have to find the editor and cover artist. You develop the blurb. You are in charge of marketing. Maybe I should say, you are in control. I've run a number of businesses and not having the numbers or speed of decision-making can be a death knell. We can move faster than anyone else! That is the power of being an indie author. All of the self-publishing skills can be learned.

Because *you* are the one to press publish, and *you* reap the rewards. Why settle for pennies on the dollar? I love to write, too, but I can manage the business aspect to garner the other 90% of revenue earned from my work. Too many say they only want to write and do none of the other things. You are selling a rather large portion of yourself by going that route. Try it yourself. You might find that it is not so daunting.

I run an indie (self-published) author group on Facebook with more than 30,000 members. It is the single best resource (in my biased opinion) for general questions and ideas on self-publishing. The 20Booksto50k® group has changed a great number of authors' lives. Hope is a powerful drug. Once you're addicted to it, you'll start to see that all things are possible.

I wrote a separate book on that stuff – Become a Successful Indie Author. I discuss the finer points that you need to address on the technical side as well as the business side. What do you need to do to get your book out there and make it start earning for you?

I love seeing my books on the shelves at Barnes & Noble, but my bread and butter come from self-publishing. In the bookstore, the spines of my novels have to compete with other spines. In cyberspace, I get to show my covers. I get to advertise to narrow audiences who read the kinds of books that I write. But once they *start* reading, will they *keep* reading?

That's compelling fiction.

Get a few books sold, get famous (or at least established), then you can break the rules.

Stephen King wrote a three-word chapter in *Misery*. Tom Wolfe wrote a four-hundred-word sentence in *Bonfire of the Vanities*. Both were (silently or at least in low tones) chastised by New York editors for "grandstanding." But they can pull off this kind of stuff because they are Stephen King and Tom Wolfe.

Consistently put a few novels on the top of the charts, and you, too, can grandstand.

Tell the story. Manage your reader expectations by giving them what they think they bought. This doesn't mean that you are selling out. Not in the least. Write what you want with an eye toward what sells. Are you a master storyteller? Of course you are. You're a human being, and we are all natural storytellers. Writing the stories, however, is a learned skill. Practice and keep practicing. The better you are, the more you'll be able to drive your story down the genre lanes of the reader road.

How long your work is matters. Many buyers are looking to get more for their money or at least a minimal number of pages. Give it to them within genre norms. What are those norms? Check the top ten lists of your genre and see. They can change week to week. On the Amazon page for a book, simply scroll down past the blurb and you'll find the page count listed in the section labeled "Product Details." Here is the Free Trader Complete Omnibus edition by Craig Martelle. Good value for your $9.99 or not?

File Size: 5957 KB
Print Length: **2206 pages**
Simultaneous Device Usage: Unlimited
Publication Date: May 23, 2019
Sold by: Amazon Digital Services LLC
Language: English
ASIN: B07S6CL35P

Whether you self-publish or go the legacy publisher route, you have to tell a good story (is that the seventh or eighth time we've said that?). You have to deliver to reader expectations. And then you have to do it again and again. That's how you make a career out of writing.

Let's get into those genre expectations and see if there are any surprises.

4

WHAT IS GENRE?

***GENRE:* Genre is defined by my Random House Dictionary as: A class or category of artistic endeavor having a particular form, content, technique, or the like.**

Let me name a few to give you context. When you browse the book racks at a Barnes & Noble, you see the headings. Besides the wide-range of non-fiction books available, romance, science fiction, horror, fantasy, thrillers, historicals, mystery, children's and westerns are all considered as separate genres—and there are more. And there are sub-genres: adult westerns, fantasy romance, post-apocalyptic, etc. You get the picture, but the main point is that readers can zero-in on the types of books they like best and from a marketing standpoint, you can zero-in on them. That also means meeting their expectations for those genres.

Who determines genre? The author first, but the author is

often wrong, unless they've written that type of novel before and know for certain. Readers who buy the books determine genre mainly through the marketplace. What I mean by that is their buying behaviors clump together books with certain stories told in a specific way. Elves and magic in a storybook setting? Maybe fantasy. Maybe Fairytales (that is a recognized sub-genre). Maybe dark fantasy or romantic fantasy. So many options, but you can get help by studying books that are similar. I use Publisher Rocket, a program by Dave Chesson and the good folks at Kindlepreneur.

In legacy publishing, acquisition editors who buy novels and guide them to finished form are focusing on a specific genre that he/she knows that they can sell to.

Readers expect such a novel, a western for instance, to be written a certain way and, because of those reader expectations, if it isn't written that way, acquisition editors generally won't buy it and readers may pan it.

If you want to sell your work to the established publishing houses, the first thing you have to realize is that publishing is a *business*. If they believe it won't sell and their sales department, cast from the same mold, believes they don't know how to sell it, they won't buy it.

With self publishing, if you want to write an alien science fiction western, go for it (check out Craig's Darklanding series, for example). The market may be tougher than a pure genre market, but who knows? You could be the one who defines the next hot genre. The greater the deviation from the main genre, the more imaginative your marketing campaign will have to be, but that's part of the fun of self-publishing. The risk may be higher, but the rewards, personal (ego) and financial can be phenomenal.

Legacy publishers want products that sell. That sounds just like self-publishers.

Genres exist with expected tropes. Romances end happily: girl gets boy and vice versa. Mysteries drip clues, and you don't know the solution until the last chapter. Sci-fi is about aliens and outer space, or inner space, including inside the body or the center of the earth. Horror had better scare the hell out of you. Since I'm concentrating on the western, crime and the historical, I'll zero in on them. And by the way, what's good for the western is generally good for the western romance, novels of the West, and historicals set in the old West. Most of it, of course, is common to all genres. Some are unique.

The same basics can be applied to all genres.

COMPARING GENRES: DIFFERENCES/SIMILARITIES BETWEEN A WESTERN AND A HISTORICAL

Random House defines a western as "a story, movie, or radio or television play about the U.S. West of the nineteenth century."

It defines a historical novel as "a narrative in novel form, characterized chiefly by an imaginative reconstruction of historical events and personages."

Let's look at those definitions as they apply to western/historical novels. And remember that a western romance may have different guidelines than those for a straight western or straight historical.

As it appears on the paperback racks in thousands of physical displays in bookstores, airports, libraries, and everywhere else you can find hard copy books along with the entirety of the internet—a western is a fictional story of forty-five to eighty-five thousand words. This is a rule. Rules are made to be broken, and the word-limit rule, like all rules in publishing, as well as most other businesses, is broken often. One of the finest western novels ever written (in my opinion, and the only Pulitzer Prize-winning western novel ever written other than Owen Wister's *The Virginian*) is much longer. We'll talk more about *Lonesome Dove* as there are a number of great lessons that demonstrate writing compelling fiction.

Again, so much for rules.

THE WESTERN GENRE

Westerns are generally set in the expansion of the West period—the year of our Lord 1840 up to the turn of the century, with by far the majority set in the twenty years from the end of the Civil War to 1885. Why? Because the reading public conceives that time frame as the "West." Buffalo Bill Cody, Wyatt Earp, Billy the Kid, cowhands, gunmen, cattle barons, Indians, Indian uprisings, the expansion of the railroads, etc., etc., were the people and the events we've come to identify with the West.

The Bureau of Census, in 1890, compiled and published *Population and Statistical Figure for The United States* and in that document declared the America frontier closed. In 1893, the Indian Territory was organized as the Oklahoma Territory and, with that act, every square inch in America was officially under some form of local government. The Wild West was over;

the frontier gone.

Stick with a story set in that time frame—the end of the Civil War to the turn of the century—at least for your first novel.

Historical? Any time in the past. Is the WW II period, or any time subsequent (say Vietnam) considered a historical time frame? It depends on the readers – if you read this genre, then you know what you expect. If you don't, then you'll find out through your advertising and marketing. Is a pre-historic considered a historical? I think most would probably consider them nearer the fantasy genre. Look at the John Jakes series of novels, *The Bastard*, etc., for my belief of what are true, easily identified historicals. And acquisition editors (if you're submitting your manuscript to legacy publishers) will know for certain if it fits with their exact definition of the genre (which is based on what they know their readers will buy). If you get rejection letters because your work is outside their boundaries, then it's time to put on your self-publishing hat and fire up your marketing engine to find other readers just like you who will like your genre. With over a billion readers of English, you will have a market as long as you don't have fatal story flaws and other things. A sound story can always be sold, but it could take a lot of work to dig out those readers.

If you want to read the most accurate and entertaining reconstruction of pre-history, read Michael and Kathleen Gear. No one writes pre-history better than a professional archeologist and anthropologist, for no one has come closer to living it.

Can a western be set in 1880's New York City, if it's about a cowhand? An eastern-western? Maybe, but I wouldn't want to try it (although it's being done in romance westerns). Talk about a hard sell (genre bending has its place, but not with legacy publishing – this could be a healthy challenge for a self-published author)! A sheriff goes after a killer in Arizona; a bad cattle baron rules the town that's grown up at the edge of his spread in New Mexico; a Union cavalry officer returns to Wyoming from the Civil War to find his sister kidnapped by the Crow. Cattle drives, gamblers and saloon girls, rustlers, robbers, Comancheros, cowboys, and Indians. These situations and characters are the meat of genre westerns.

But western romances, historicals, and contemporary novels with western settings can be written with much greater leeway.

SETTING:

Setting? Set your western or historical in the West or, if a historical, preferably in a place you know a lot about. If not your own home town, then a place you've visited and, hopefully, learned something about its history. Not absolutely necessary, but helpful. It's hard enough to break into a new business. Make it as easy on yourself as possible.

My first book was about my home town, Bakersfield, California. It was a hard sell. Even though the West's greatest stock drive originated in Kern County, and one of the last great shootouts took place in the Bakersfield Tenderloin, New York editors think of the West as Abilene, Tombstone, Fort Worth, Santa Fe, Rawlins, etc. These are the places they've read about in westerns for years. Except for the gold rush period, they think of California as the land of fruits and nuts. Mark Twain said California was "West of the West," and New York still believes it to a great extent.

If I were starting my first book again, I would set it in an area deemed western by the folks who buy these books—acquisition editors and readers.

But again, this is a rule that has been successfully broken. What you need to know about a setting can be researched in the local library. Tom Clancy wrote his best-selling, *The Hunt for Red October*, set almost entirely in a nuclear submarine involving intricate detail, and he'd never set foot in a nuclear sub.

It can be done; it's just tougher.

And here again, settings for western romances, historicals, and other genres utilizing western themes are much broader and much less limiting than genre westerns.

These rules will be more easily and more often broken now that acquisition editors are out of the picture thanks to self publishing. We've removed the gatekeepers, and now the sky is the limit.

As long as you've written compelling fiction. We have some great lessons from westerns that cross into all genres. Always write a great story, no matter whether it's a western set in New York City or in Tombstone.

STORY:

What's a western about? Generally it's a drama. If you want to write a book about the trials and tribulations of a comic watchmaker who happens to live in Santa Fe in 1875, you'd better make him the toughest watchmaker in several states, who defends his watches to the death with a Colt .44 and a bowie knife!

A drama is defined by Random House as:

A composition in prose or verse presenting in dialogue or pantomime a story involving conflict or contrast of character...any situation or series of events having vivid, emotional, conflicting, or striking interest or results.

A good western, like any good drama, is about trial and tribulation, success and failure, and riveting head-to-head conflict.

The finest compliment a novelist can get is "I read your book in one sitting." Even if they hated it, it was compelling! A "page turner." Let me qualify that compliment by reminding you that generally westerns are short. Other than an insomniac speed reader, no one could read *War and Peace* in one sitting. That your book is compelling is the greatest compliment a writer can get.

Conflict and its resolution create compelling reading. Put your hero up a cliff, out of powder, wad, and shot, hostile Indians below, a rabid cougar on the cliff above, and a grizzly protecting her cubs in the cave behind—and your hero developing a migraine. See *Raiders of the Lost Ark* as an example.

Now that's compelling reading!

An obvious exaggeration. We'll talk about credibility—and pacing—later, but you get the idea.

Set your western or historical anywhere you love to read about and study, for you'll have to know a lot about time and place to write a successful one. It helps to pick a location and time that has been written about by good historians.

And then there's the space westerns. Look at *Darklanding* by Craig Martelle and Scott Moon. Touted as a space western, what do you think of this scene? Does it set the stage with sufficient conflict and drama?

Thaddeus Fry, Sheriff of Darklanding, opened the door and walked in to the Mother Lode, a saloon from another era where people and aliens alike gathered to forget their woes.

And go deeper in debt to the Company.

The clash of noise and light stopped Thad in his tracks. He blinked and winced at the assault upon his senses. He oriented himself and headed straight for the bar. The bartender looked at him sideways, but didn't speak.

"I'm supposed to have a room here," Thad said matter-of-factly.

After a long hesitation, the man replied, "Rooms are handled at the front desk." He jabbed a finger toward a desk on the other side of the bar. It couldn't be seen from the front door, and there was no sign.

Thad thought about telling the bartender that questions could be allayed with a little effort, but bringing that up wasn't his concern. Never volunteer, a lesson he learned in the army, applied to fixing other people's problems. They might not see them as problems and any fixes would be seen as an intrusion.

"Obliged. Thank you." Thad moved to the empty desk and stood there. There wasn't a bell to ring. He suspected his presence would alert someone to do their job.

Shortly, the bartender arrived and took a seat behind the desk. "How can I help you?" he asked gruffly.

Thad held his gaze steady, torn between rolling his eyes and grabbing the man by the throat.

Sometimes, you just have to revel in the absurdity of it all.

"My orders show that I'm billeted here. Temporarily, that is." Thad handed over his pad with the orders prominently displayed.

The man's face dropped as he recited the first line. "Sheriff Thaddeus Fry."

The sheriff had blocked out the sounds from the saloon, but the sudden silence was as loud as a rifle shot. He turned to see a variety of faces looking at him. From their seats at the gaming tables, from the dancers on stage, from the restaurant at the far end, to others drinking by themselves, all eyes were on him.

That's science fiction and a book that resonated well with readers of that genre. Similar scenes played out in many a Louis L'Amour novel. Lessons from westerns can be universal.

SEX:

Sex? The "S" word. In the last few years, the "adult western," with explicit sock-it-to-'em, a-different-lady-in-each-chapter sex, has developed its own audience, and it's a fairly big one as genre writing goes. It's still not the norm. The rule is: The only one kissed by the hero in a western is his horse. Like the other rules, this one was made to be broken. Romance is part of life, and I try to include a little of it in all my novels. And a lot in some.

There is a romantic interest in most, if not all, of Louis L'Amour's novels. Romance, as Zane Grey so aptly put it, is idealism, and westerns, as Louis L'Amour so aptly wrote them, are about the dignity of western man. Ideals. Romance. Good triumphs over evil. The good guy wins.

Keep explicit sex (vivid description) to your mainstream, contemporary, romance, or even erotica book if the heat level is too high. If you want to sell your western as a classic western, then keep it to a simmer. A historical offers greater leeway. See Ken Follett as an example.

I try to limit the sex in my books to the dropping of a boot or the closing of a bedroom door. Kat writes romance, so don't read her books unless you are ready to break out in a sweat. But (to her credit in my way of thinking) sex in her novels is always between consenting adults and 99.99% of the time between adults who are married or eventually will be.

The above does not mean there's not a market for an explicitly sexy western. It's a different target audience, that's all. Know your genre cold and then it's much easier to market and find the right readers.

THE ENDING:

I only include this subject in this section because some genres have definite ending requirements. For example, a romance novel must end happily—boy gets girl (or girl gets boy!). A mystery must end with a solution to the mystery. But a western, historical, or thriller can end in any way.

High Noon ended happily. *Shane* rode off into the sunset, alone and without attachments again—happiness for the settler whose wife he was so attracted too, but not the generally accepted happy ending. There is no hard and fast rule. *Open Range*, one of the better later westerns, ends happily. Open Range was the name of the movie, but it was based on a book titled "The Open Range Men" by Lauran Paine. As well, High Noon was based on "The Tin Star" by John W. Cunningham.

But generally a western ends like *High Noon* or *Shane*, or somewhere between the two.

The hard quiet stranger, triumphant but alone, who rides off into the unknown is usually the saddest of western endings. Why? Because most of us want to feel good. When the last trooper of the cavalry regiment and the last Indian from the village kill each other with their last bullets while standing on top of a pile of trooper and Indian bodies—characters a good writer has brought you to care about—you've got a sad ending. There's a market for it, but it's not my cup of tea.

Write a *Shane* or *High Noon* ending and you'll sell your first western novel.

A historical can end in any fashion. Again, it offers much more leeway.

So, what's a western?

An exciting, compelling drama that takes place between 1840 and 1885, about the West, with a hero who prevails and wins the lady's love, or at least respect and yearning, and saves the town, ranch, railroad, stage coach line, etc., etc...

But, hell's bells, if you get right down to it, your guess is as good as mine. Just end on a high note of some sort. Westerns like winners, but winners can define what that means. Maybe the ranch was burned down and the horses run off, but the rustlers are done for and our hero can rebuild in peace with the love of the town supporting him for running off the riffraff.

Write a novel the readers can't put down. A compelling conflict. The West, the East, the North, or South at its glorious best and evil worst.

Let us throw out a few specifics from other genres, only to make general points. We'll keep these sections short, while diving deep into the westerns and science fiction. Rehashing the same lessons, will waste your time. There are subtle differences and a great deal of overlap. I think you'll see the points as we continue.

There are many ways to study individual genres, but what you'll find is each one is unique in a certain way that attracts readers to that particular type of story.

Read your genre and study it. See what the books in the top ten are doing. How are they different, but more importantly, how are they the same? And then look at how the lessons we're showing here resonate across them all.

THE HISTORICAL GENRE

The historical is basically any novel set in the past. What is the exact time break that divides a historical from a contemporary? Generally a contemporary is set now. A historical is set in the past. Is the Vietnam era "the past?" It depends on the reader's interpretation. I would say *Winds of War* is a historical, set in WW II. John Jakes's great series, *The Bastard*, etc., etc., is the best example of true historicals I can give. James Michener's *Hawaii, Chesapeake*, and *Centennial* are great examples. James Clavell's *Tai-Pan* and *Shogun* are also among the finest of the genre. There are also historical romances, and many sub-genres thereof; and historicals that dig all the way back to prehistoric times—some of which, like *Clan of the Cave Bear* have been tremendously popular. And that novel began a new sub-genre. The Gears, Kathleen and Michael, picked up that gauntlet and improved upon it.

Basically the difference between a historical novel set in the old West—(some call it a novel of the West)—and a western, is length. A historical should be around 130,000 words, or twice as long as a western.

My novel, *Rush to Destiny*, is a historical. It's just over 130,000 words. It's based on the early life of Edward Fitzgerald Beale. I'll tell you more about Beale and the writing of *Rush to Destiny* when we talk in depth about "writing from history"—and that might as well be now.

THE CRIME/THRILLER/MYSTERY NOVEL

Grisham says these are the rules he followed when he began writing:

10 Rules From Suspense Fiction
by Brian Garfield

1. Start with action, explain it later
2. Make it tough for your protagonist
3. Plant it early, pay it off later
4. Give the protagonist the initiative
5. Give the protagonist a personal stake
6. Give the protagonist a tight time limit, then shorten it (ticking clock)
7. Choose your character according to your own capacities, as well as his
8. Know your destination before you set out
9. Don't rush in where angels fear to tread
10. Don't write anything you wouldn't want to read

The crime novel is, obviously, about a crime or crimes. Unlike a mystery, a crime novel does not have to have the perpertrator revealed until the end. Crime novels can use standard police procedures or how the protagonist gets around them to achieve the desired end state.

A thriller normally has a much broader spectrum and more at risk than a crime or mystery novel. It's the dirty bomb in L.A. Harbor, or the spreading of ricin in the subway. Thrillers also have a certain action level – something must happen with great enough frequency to keep the readers engaged. James Patterson has written thrillers with some kind of action on every single page. Others are every four pages, but once every thirteen pages is the least amount of action to remain within the thriller and action genres.

A mystery is just that, usually a crime in the first chapter, a plethora of clues along the way, and its solving in the last chapter.

SCIENCE FICTION

This is the beauty of science fiction. The future. A reimagined past. A dystopian present. Some science involved. Definitely fiction, but not necessarily. When George Orwell wrote *1984*, he envisioned a future that has seen too many of his elements come true. In Star Trek, much of what you see on the small screen now exists in real life. Science Fiction is a wide open genre. Reach for the stars.

The future of science or is it the limits of imagination? Neither and both. Science fiction is a rich genre that has a broad range of sub-genres like military science fiction, space opera, hard science fiction, alien contact, galactic colonization. Space ships. Distant planets. Fantastic technologies.

I'll tell you a secret. Just like in westerns, when all is said and done, the story is about the characters. There are oddities and one-offs, but the vast majority of science fiction is about the people. This is what the readers don't know that they expect. They want worldbuilding that they can embrace. Frank Herbert's *Dune* is a massive universe with many moving parts. Frank was the master of it and shared bits and pieces of it with his readers. Once he passed away, his son Brian and master storyteller Kevin J. Anderson continued writing books in that universe. Nineteen books and counting, plus a new movie. The most compelling science fiction creates a strong universe as the backdrop upon which the characters act.

That's science fiction, along with so much more.

It starts with an imagined world, whether that is today, but different and then builds out a plot that could come from that same world of today. Science fiction opens up possibilities of what if. Very much like we see in westerns, the universal plot device of "What if?" It works.

URBAN FANTASY

Take Urban Fantasy like Harry Potter. This is a huge genre with hungry readers across all age groups looking for the next big thing. If you love JK Rowling's works, then maybe you have an Urban Fantasy story to tell. What if *you* had a magic high school?

Urban Fantasy has romantic elements in it. There is magic. Usually those who use magic don't necessarily know the extent of their gifts. Is Urban Fantasy always about teenagers? Not necessarily, but many are.

Look at the emerging magic academy and school books. Hundreds of authors are plunging into this genre in 2018 and 2019. What makes them stand out? Covers with greens and purples. Lead characters with the magic hands. Something mystical going on in the background. Those points draw the readers into the blurb. Is the hook there to make the reader go further?

Only the reader will know. Conversion rates – the rate at which clicks on your ad turn into sales of your book are the best determinant of how well your cover and blurb work to turn readers into buyers.

What kind of journey will the reader join as part of this magical adventure? Journey. Antagonist. Protagonist. Conflict. Resolution. The same, but different.

See a pattern here?

OTHER GENRES

We won't write much about other genres as we don't write them, other than a few nonfiction works such as the one you're reading, or *How To Build A Greenhouse, Killing Cancer, Cooking Wild and Wonderful* or *California Cocina.* If you write nonfiction, write something you know and are hopefully an expert at accomplishing.

5

THE PROCESS

A novel is a fictional story with a beginning, middle, and end. It has characters, plot, time, and place. The trick is to bring those elements together in a compelling read.

Lonesome Dove, by Larry McMurtry, is the story of a cattle drive. It begins in Texas and ends in Montana—and takes months. Simple. Straightforward. A Pulitzer Prize winner. No complicated flashbacks to deal with. Your western can be a journey. Or it can be another kind of quest—the sheriff goes after the killer or vice versa. *High Noon* takes place in one town, in one afternoon. By the way, the movie was based on a great short story, *The Tin Star*, by John M. Cunningham.

Both plots are filled with drama. Drama in every scene. Conflict in every scene. Conflict in every scene, because drama *is* conflict, and a scene is not a scene without conflict of some sort. I'm going to repeat that, because it's a critical part of writing compelling novels. There is no scene without conflict.

And the above, as to drama and conflict holds true for every genre of fiction.

Even a romance, ending happily ever after, must have conflict in every scene. Much of the conflict in romance is sexual tension.

CONFLICT:

Conflict can be man/woman against man, man against the elements, man against animal, man against woman, or man against himself. Here are a few scene setters that are examples of conflict – quick and straightforward.

- *A man parked his car and got out, making a beeline for the house. A woman blocked the doorway, her fists jammed into her hips.*
- *The player threw his cards on the table and snarled at the dealer.*
- *The grizzly's face appeared through the brush at the edge of the campfire's light. The old man slowly moved his hand toward the pistol in his coat pocket while wondering if it would do any good against the massive beast.*
- *Terry Henry stood at the precipice and looked down. He needed to get to the other side, but there was no bridge.*
- *The young man gently traced a single finger down the side of her face. Her breath caught as her lips parted.*
- *"Will you go to the dance with me?" Crivner asked.*

Her look of horror gave him his answer before she opened her mouth.

- *Knuckles white from clenching, Lafferty couldn't relax. His lip twisted, and he leaned forward. Unbalanced, he lashed out anyway. The young punk easily dodged the blow, stepping in to his counterpunch like an old pro.*

Your story is about your hero overcoming one or all of them. No one wants to read about a pleasant cattle drive across grass-filled plains dotted with water holes in wonderful weather where everyone gets along famously. Or, to be more succinct, *where nothing happens.* Boring!

Conflict and its resolution make compelling reading.

Every scene must have conflict of some kind or it shouldn't be in your story. If there's no conflict, then it's only a transition, getting your story from one place or another or from one time to another. A transition deserves no more than a paragraph, usually at the beginning or ending of a scene.

Here's an example of conflict from a science fiction novel.

Judge, Jury, & Executioner 6 – *Fratricide* by Craig Martelle. Here's a scene up front that sets the stage.

"You're the safety guy on this project. What the hell is wrong with you?" The construction superintendent wasn't amused. He put his back to the window, crossed his arms, and glared at his safety manager.

"We have the latest processes and procedures in place. The overall risk for any job undertaken by a human or alien is low. Every fucking one is low!"

"Five dead bodies suggest you're wrong."

Boran ran his hand through his hair. He was as upset as anyone. It was his job to ensure the safety of the crew. It was his job to make sure they were complying with procedures. And it was his personal responsibility because he insisted on it.

He sat, his head bowed and shoulders hunched like the defeated man he was. "I did everything right," he mumbled into his hands, his mind racing as it had ever since the first accident trying to figure out why. "You can have my resignation."

"Shut your soup sucker!" the superintendent blurted. "You are going to figure this out. When the Fed's Magistrate arrives, we're all going to meet her at the airlock and you're going to escort her and her team everywhere they want to go. You'll arrange anything they want, from casual conversations to negotiations to catered lunches. And you'll stick with them until they're done. If they learn anything, you'll pass that to me as soon as possible, understand?"

"So, I'm a servant and a spy?" Boran wasn't amused, but he had already surrendered. He accepted the premise that no one would ever hire a safety manager with five accidental deaths to his name.

"You are anything I want you to be since I'm paying you. Yes. Spy. Servant. Safety guy."

Conflict doesn't have to be in your face. Here's something from Anne McCaffrey (Dragon Riders of Pern)

"The bronze rider of Mnementh, Lord F'lar, will require quarters for himself. I, F'nor, brown rider, prefer to be lodged with the wingmen. We are, in number, twelve." F'lar liked that touch of F'nor's, totting up the wing strength, as if Fax were incapable of counting.

Or sometimes it is in your face. From Craig Martelle's *Free Trader of Warren Deep*,

'Ass!'

"You are such an ass!" Braden lay by the fire in the blanket he'd been using since he was a child. The young man's long braid was wrapped around his neck like a scarf. He looked at the Hillcat, a scowl darkening his face.

'It makes noises but no sense,' the 'cat responded over their mindlink. The 'cat's orange back, even with a man's knee, had black dots and a black slash toward his tail. He was called a Hellcat by those who'd seen him make a kill, but not by Braden, his most loyal friend.

See the opening – a conflict and dichotomy that sets the stage for eleven more books. His most loyal friend and they argue like a married couple. How about the opening line of Dickens' *A Tale of Two Cities*?

It was the best of times, it was the worst of times, it was the age of wisdom, it was the age of foolishness, it was the epoch of belief, it was the epoch of incredulity, it was the season of light, it was the season of darkness, it was the spring of hope, it was the winter of despair.

Conflict creating the desire to know more. So good.

How about Craig Martelle's Nightwalker 5?

Wolfe shouldered his AR-15 and watched for movement in the distance. The young girl, Jennifer was curled up with the big German Shepherd-Wolf mix, Buddy. The two were inseparable and reminded him every day what he was fighting for.

What is the conflict in that opening line? A girl and a dog were sleeping, yet the protector was armed and ready to fight for them. Simple but keeps the readers turning the page. Drama that promises action.

PLOTTING:

There are thousands of variations on plot. Plot, by the way, is defined by my trusty Random House dictionary thus:

....Also called storyline, the plan, scheme, or main story of a literary or dramatic work [*such*] *as a play, novel, or short story.*

There's that word *drama* again. And remember this: the definition of drama included the words *character* and *conflict.*

According to Christopher Booker, all fiction can be categorized within seven (nine) plots.

1. Overcoming the monster (or mega villain – James Bond films, or Clash of the Titans)
2. Rags to riches (King Arthur, Cinderella)
3. Quest (Lord of the Rings, Indiana Jones)
4. Voyage and Return (Wizard of Oz, Gulliver's Travels)
5. Comedy (when plots are designed around the humor)
6. Tragedy (think Shakespeare)
7. Rebirth (Beauty and the Beast, The Secret Garden)
8. Mystery (Sherlock Holmes, Agatha Christie)
9. Rebellion against the one (Booker says this is like Hunger Games, but he isn't sure it is a plot that is alone, but rather a combination of others)

So your plot, whether it be a journey or a quest, has character and conflict. Your job is to fill two hundred pages of words with compelling characters and hard-hitting conflict if you're writing a western, and five hundred and twenty pages if you're writing a historical novel.

Drama! That's what you're after.

How? By telling a story.

A story of conflict.

Some writers sit down with pencil and paper, or at the typewriter, or in front of a computer, and begin writing. Others plan carefully. Either way, in order to begin, it helps to have your basic story in mind. Think it through first—at least the main plot points.

I'm a character-driven writer. I like to create interesting characters and let them run with the story. Kat, my wife, is a plot-driven writer. She knows exactly where her story is going when she sits down and types "Chapter One." Neither of us is right or wrong. What works for you is right.

Thankfully, most westerns have simple plots. One hero or protagonist; one or more villains or antagonists. A journey or quest. Seldom does a western have an intricate plot or subplot. Seldom are flashbacks used. The drama moves forward in a straight time line.

A historical, on the other hand, can be much more complex.

Science fiction or Fantasy? Wide open. Think of the Hero's Journey, Sam and Frodo going on an epic journey to destroy the One Ring. There are an infinite number of obstacles, but them as they come to them. Lord of the Rings never would have worked from a first person POV. How could it have been a tale of epically sweeping proportions if we were limited to the world as seen through Frodo's eyes. We would have missed fully a half of the trilogy.

If you want more information on plotting, there are some excellent resources – *Take Off Your Pants* by Libbie Hawker and *Save the Cat! Writes a Novel* by Jessica Brody. Another great resource is John Truby's *The Anatomy of Story*.

Because plotting and point of view (POV) are so entwined, I'll continue the plotting discussion as we talk about POV.

POINT OF VIEW (POV):

I've got a point of view about most subjects. So do you; so does your mother-in-law. But that's not the kind of *point of view* we're talking about.

After an acquisition editor or the reading public discovers that you've written a novel with prose, a good plot, and characters who come alive, the next thing a good editor does is to turn his or her attention to point of view. More basically good novels are trashed because of inconsistent point of view than for any other technical reason.

Point of view—through whose eyes the story is seen—is a determinate of plot. For the sake of simplicity, we'll begin with the first person. You can't wander away from the direct line-of-sight view or hearing of the storyteller if you write your novel in the first person—that is the "I" point of view.

I made sure my Walker rode free and easy in the holster as the cackler rose from his ladder back chair. (That's first person.)

Ethan hoisted his Walker, making sure it rode free and easy, as the cackler rose from the ladder back chair. (That's third person.)

If the point of view then shifts to the cackler, then to the barmaid across the room, it's third person omniscient—the all-seeing eye. I chose to use the third person omni POV in some of my writing, first person in other novels, and a combination in some.

Should I choose omni in this example, I could go on to begin the next paragraph, or next chapter:

Meanwhile, back at the ranch....

You can't do that in first person. You can't go to the ranch in your writing unless you take your first person along. Simple? No, it's not simple for me. I still fight proper POV every time I write, but at least now, when someone asks me "What's your point of view?" I don't launch into a political observation or my opinion about the last news story on the tube.

Point of view, as it applies to the craft of writing, is where you place your camera. *Is it behind the eyes of a single character or in the corner of a room where it can see all?*

Before you plot your novel, you must determine how you will write the point of view. A first person POV cannot have flashbacks unless the protagonist (99% of all first person novels are written from the hero's POV) is the one thinking about the flashback. A first person POV cannot see or hear something that's happening in the next room, next building, or next town. It limits your plot—or at least your approach to your plot. For that reason, most novels and certainly most westerns and historicals are written in third person omniscient (omni).

Third person omni is defined as where the narrator knows the thoughts and feelings of all the characters in the story. There's also third person limited, which is the pure camera view from the corner of the room. There is no look inside the heads of the characters. Everything is limited to what is seen, said, and done. There are no forays into thoughts or internal emotions. Third person limited challenges the author to show not tell. It can work well, but if you need to show any kind of a character's internal dialogue, then you'll need to stick with omni.

Can you change your point of view in a novel? Of course you can. Most writers change not only in the novel but within individual scenes. I suggest you don't change in a given paragraph; in fact, I wouldn't change without changing scenes. But you can go from your hero's point of view to your heroine's and back.

Look at *End Times Alaska*, this is the only series that I (Craig) have written in first person POV but it is in the post-apocalyptic/survivalist genre. Remember our conversation above about genre norms? It is typical to write PA novels in first person. That was a bestselling series because it delivered to reader expectations. It was the right story for that traditional publisher (an imprint of Simon & Schuster) for their audience. But it limited how the plot folded. Or did it? There are chapters in third person omni, because there were parallel sub-plots and the books were written chronologically. But the POV was consistent within the chapter. It only changed with a new chapter, if that's where the story needed to go.

We have read and written successful novels in both the first person and other points of view. (A difficult approach for a beginning writer, and probably difficult for most readers to read and acquisition editors to accept.)

Decide your POV and then move to the plot.

DESCRIPTION:

I can't think of a faster way to get me to put a novel down than to layer in too much laborious description. Many writers and many readers love a novel dripping...no, *gushing*...description. Many writers are great at purple prose, but give me a lean one every time.

A few years ago I read *The Bridges of Madison County* by Robert James Waller, a small hardback which had a modest first printing—but a book that had *legs*, as they say in the trade. The book was on the *Publisher's Weekly* bestseller list for hundreds of weeks. And the reason is that it says a great deal in its 171 pages, with a number of great similes and metaphors. When you're writing about unrequited love, and your character is aging with "dust on his heart," as Mr. Waller's protagonist did, you don't have to say a lot more.

Remember brevity: read *The Bridges of Madison County* and find it at its best. I'm a fan of Stephen King and Dean Koontz, but of all their novels I've enjoyed, I like King's *Misery* and Koontz's *Intensity* better than any of their other works. Why? Brevity. They're among the shortest of their novels. Packed with impact, if I may, with the conflict coming at you fast and furiously. Read both for a lesson in suspense, then read them again, because the first time you'll be so taken up with the story you'll forget to analyze the writing.

However, if we're talking fantasy, then in depth descriptions with seemingly extreme numbers of adjectives are what the readers expect. Take this from Robert E. Howard & L. Sprague De Camp's, *Queen of the Black Coast*

"I have known many gods. He who denies them is as blind as he who trusts them too deeply. I seek not beyond death. It may be the blackness averred by the Nemedian skeptics, or Crom's realm

of ice and cloud, or the snowy plains and vaulted halls of the Nordheimer's Valhalla. I know not, nor do I care. Let me live deep while I live; let me know the rich juices of red meat and stinging wine on my palate, the hot embrace of white arms, the mad exultation of battle when the blue blades flame and crimson, and I am content. Let teachers and philosophers brood over questions of reality and illusion. I know this: if life is illusion, then I am no less an illusion, and being thus, the illusion is real to me. I live, I burn with life, I love, I slay, and am content."

DESCRIPTION THROUGH POINT OF VIEW:

Do you remember that I keep a sign over my desk that says "filter all description though point of view." Why? Because by *not* doing so, you're engaging in *author intrusion*. By *doing* so, you give your reader a great insight into the minds of your characters. Let me show you what I mean.

Miss Mary Jane Petersen crossed the boardwalk and paused in front of the batwing doors. Taking a tentative breath, then a deep one, she smoothed her linen skirt. Finally, boldly, back stiff and chin held high, she entered.

The room, filled with bawdy men, reeking of tobacco smoke and sweat, stopped her short. The clamor silenced as all eyes turned to her—but she was careful not to meet them. She strode on, moving to the plank bar and finding the gaze of the curious barkeep.

"Your proprietor. Mr. Oscar Tidwell, please," she said, carefully keeping her voice from cracking.

Or:

Miss Mary Jane Petersen crossed the board walk and paused

in front of the batwing doors. Tucking her loose fitting blouse in tightly—purposefully straining it against her ample bosom, which she had long known was her best feature—she pushed boldly into the saloon. The smell of working men always made her pocketbook itch, and now was no different.

Bawdy men paused and surveyed her as she strode across the room to the plank bar, then went back to their faro and poker and whiskey.

The barkeep shined a mug as she approached. He, too, let his eyes drift to the straining fabric. It was all she could do not to smile. Men were so simply manipulated.

"The boss, please...Mr. Tidwell."

Do you get two different opinions about Miss Mary Jane—even though the bar scene is basically the same? By describing the room and its occupants through her point of view, we understand the character.

Some see the glass as half empty, some as half full. Some see the roses, some only the thorns.

PACING:

A quick look at pacing before we begin to write. If readers want conflict, give them conflict—a story with high emotion! But, caution, no one wants a single emotion read. By that I mean your plot has to have pacing. If your hero wakes up facing a band of hostile warriors, escapes them to run into a grizzly, and escapes it to be chased by wolves—it's a single-emotion read and will be no more compelling than the cattle drive where nothing happened.

You want to build emotion, throughout the novel, to the

climax. A series of conflicts is fine, in fact necessary, but intersperse them with a few relaxed reflective moments at the campfire. He's (or she's) in trouble; he's out; he's in deeper; he's out; he's in deeper yet, until the conclusion when he's home free. A great method to create compelling reading is to constantly throw your hero into deeper and deeper trouble, but paced with reflective scenes between scenes of action. The calm points are critical for the reader to catch their breath.

Take yoga, for example. I know, an odd reference for two old dudes who write books, but bear with me. The poses are held for thirty seconds to a minute and then one must relax. The poses are repeated a few times and then there's a longer break before the practitioner moves into a new position. It is natural for a body to need down time between tension. This is why a marathon is so challenging. Look at any professional sport. It cannot be all action all the time. There are breaks. It is how our bodies are conditioned. Reading is no different.

Kat and I both subscribe to the Syd Field method of pacing. Field is the author of a great book on how to write a screenplay. Kat and I have attended his screenplay seminar and I suggest that any writer of screenplays *or* novels does the same if he's still teaching. If not, buy his books. Much of what he teaches is applicable to the novel. He structures screenplays into segments, with the segment break being a "plot point." A plot point is ***a major change in the direction the action is moving***, generally as it directly affects your hero.

In the movie, *An Officer and a Gentleman,* the first plot point (almost always about twenty-seven minutes into the movie) is when the hero is accepted into the service. The second major plot point (twenty-seven minutes from the end of the movie) is when he decides to quit. Just about the time the viewer might become bored with the chain of events, which are somewhat constant, the writer throws a zinger at him, and his interest is renewed. You can take almost any successful movie and, with stop watch in hand, see that it follows Field's paradigm—a theory I'm sure he developed from doing just that—watching successful movies. There are many other rules to follow, including the midpoints, the beginning ten minutes, etc., etc., but I'll let his book teach you those. Here's how it applies to your novel.

Just about the time your reader is in the groove—the hero and heroine have fallen madly in love and are to be married tomorrow—it's time to have her kidnapped and dragged away. A major change in events; a shock to renew reader interest.

Pacing is all important to compelling writing.

CHARACTER NAMES:

This is an opportunity to shape the impression of your character without having to go into an extended description. Whether readers admit it or not, they will generalize based on their pre-conceived notions. I wouldn't name my western hero Percy. Not that Percy's not a nice name, but it connotes an English butler to me. If my hero's an English butler, then Percy is fine.

A master of names was Tom Donbavand. In one of his science fiction novels, his protagonist was Captain Jack Marber and the antagonist was Vimor Malfic. See how they give you an impression.

"I'm Terry Henry Walton, but my friends call me TH."

I once asked Tommy D what his secret was to naming characters and here's what he told me.

I did what I normally do - find an Earth plant or animal with a passing connection to what I'm trying to come up with and find inspiration in their Latin classification names. I don't take directly from those words, but twist and adapt them until they sound real enough. I stayed clear of obvious puns (Robin Birdwing, Manta Ray, Digger Dust, etc.) Here's what I came up with for your High Priestess character.

No animals or plants have priests (to our knowledge!), but bees do have Queens. So, I bastardized a few words from bee species and came up with a couple of single word names and a few two word names. As with everything, these can be tweaked, twisted and rearranged into more pleasingly sounding names should you wish.

Melifera
Scutelfa
Lingaria
Menachil
Collet Halcin
Dapsy Stenotride
Adreni Apida

What about names from non-English backgrounds? You can target a demographic by using a name from that language. In my Terry Henry Walton Chronicles, the co-protagonist's name is Charumati. A fan vehemently argued against the picture we had on the cover because the name was Indian (South Asian). My character wasn't. I simply liked the name. I explained it in the text, but if you have to explain something that could be misleading, then you are setting your readers up to stop reading. Don't give them any reason to put your story down.

In this case, the internet is your friend. Search for names, baby names, Indian names, European names, and anything else you can think of. There are lists on top of lists. I've copied a lot of them into a separate file for personal use. I think I have twenty or thirty thousand names at my fingertips. You can easily do the same thing.

Another hint about names that's important. It's tough enough to follow a novel, particularly one you pick up and put down, without having an author name a couple of primary characters Eloise and Elliott. Use the alphabet and don't set out to confuse readers. Make it as easy on them as you can by naming characters with easily identifiable handles. Name them Able, Bart, Charles, Darwin, Elliott, Ferdinand....get the picture.

If you're writing historicals, use names from the time period. Jed and Isaac, for instance, were common names in the mid-1800s and connote a feeling of time and place to the reader.

Science fiction takes greater liberties with names creating many that are unpronounceable by the human tongue. But your reader has to pronounce them as he or she will be reading the names. We may not have aliens named Bob, but we could have B'ob'ik. Looks alien but the reader can visualize the name without being too cumbersome even if the apostrophes are supposed to represent glottal stops. A technique that Craig uses for names in his stories is to ask his fans. He'll put out a call in social media, a direct link with his fanbase for names for certain character types, and his fans deliver dozens within minutes and hundreds within hours. It is a smorgasbord to choose from.

We also don't name every character. Sometimes, a character

is simply there. They don't have a role that deserves taking up a reader's brain space. Keep this in mind before you deliver a laundry list of names as if you're reciting Genesis, which could be a respectable source of biblical names for that Amish Cyberpunk novel you've thought about writing.

But avoid the stylistic approach of lines and lines of begets.

From a technical standpoint, use an easy to type name for your protagonist or as a computer hack, use something unique that you can use the find/replace function on. djk is quick and easy to type. When you search for it, they come up. Then simply replace djk with whatever the name is. Just remember your placeholders and make sure you're consistent. Your computer won't find dkl and your copyeditor will wonder if you've had a stroke when they review your work.

Names are an important part of every story. Adding them haphazardly will look just like that. But if you go into it with forethought, you'll bolster your story, add depth to your characters, and keep the narrative moving forward in the direction you wish.

LET'S WRITE:

The scene below is an example of a piece (intended to be a genre western) in the early stages of writing. As we proceed, we'll look at some improvements. At the end of the book, I'll offer a polished version. But every novel has to have a beginning:

The town, and the saloon, looked friendly enough. But looks deceive.

Ethan dismounted and loosened the cinch so the lathered

roan could catch its breath. Mopping the sweat from his brow with the back of his hand, Ethan glanced at the afternoon sky. Indian summer, still no sign of storm. But it would come. Digging a handful of grain out of a saddlebag, he offered it in his palm. The big roan mouthed it as Ethan scratched the horse's ears with his free hand. All the while, he listened for sounds from inside the Laramie Queen.

A cool beer would suit him before he resupplied at the mercantile with his last three dollars then rode on out of town to camp alone on the banks of the Laramie River. With luck and easy country, tomorrow he would make the banks of the Medicine Bow.

Luck hadn't been exactly doggin' his trail for the last thousand miles. He'd been gnawing the last of his venison jerky and drinking trail coffee made from scorched, stoneground mesquite beans for two weeks.

Getting some real grub would suit him fine. But trouble wouldn't suit him, and trouble had a way of following him.

No sound came from inside, so Ethan tied the roan to the hitching post near a wooden water trough and watched as the big horse muzzled aside some floating green moss and began to drink deeply. From habit, Ethan hoisted the heavy old Walker Colt .44 an inch, making sure it rode free and easy in its holster. He knocked the dust, billowing into the still air, from his breeches with his broad brimmed Palo Alto hat. Only then did Ethan clank across the board porch and enter the batwing doors.

The jingling of his big roweled Spanish spurs and the echoing of his footfalls on the mud, smashed-eggshell, and broken-crock-covered floor announced his entry. The room reeked of dust, sweat-soaked men, and cigar smoke.

From across the rough plank bar, the bartender gave the dusty stranger a tight smile. "Beer?"

The trail-tough cowhand rubbed the black whisker stubble on his chin with a knotted callused hand. "That'll do," Ethan said, and laid a nickel on the rough plank.

A horse fly buzzed around, inspecting the coin, as Ethan waited.

The bartender set the mug in front of him without comment, then snatched up the nickel. As Ethan took a deep draw, he heard shrill drunken laughter from a table in the back of the tall narrow room. Backhanding the foam from his handlebar mustache, Ethan cut his eyes.

Four men sat playing poker under a wafting cloud of cigar smoke. One of them, the cackler, was the Bantam rooster who—with five riders to back him up—had forced Ethan to backtrack twenty miles and ride around the Lazy A.

That's a beginning, of sorts. Not the best beginning, not the worst. Your hero walks, alone and moving West, into a Laramie saloon and is goaded into a gunfight by the town tough. He kills the young tough in a shootout. The youth turns out to be the son of the most powerful man in the county. The hero was in trouble when the tough began goading him; now he's in deeper trouble. The friendly saloon girl informs him that the sheriff is due back anytime, and the sheriff is the cattle baron's nephew and the cousin of the man he killed. He's in deeper and deeper. Even though he was in the right, he'd better run. He gets away but, sitting high on a ridge, spots a large group of riders coming his way. A posse. Deeper and deeper. He didn't have a chance to gather provisions in town, and he's low on beans and bullets. Deeper and deeper. The first storm of the year is rolling in, and he can't light a fire. Deeper and deeper and deeper.

You get the idea.

This method works for sci-fi—watch any *Star Trek* episode—for romance, for horror, for historicals, and on and on.

Characterization is equally important. For the reader to get involved in your plot and care about it, he has to care about your characters. Caring is emotion—love or hate or something in between.

Generally, you want your reader to love, or certainly admire and respect, your hero, or most aspects of your hero; and hate, or dislike most aspects of your villain. Sometimes, a good plot twist is to blur the lines, when your villain has traits that you like. Take great care giving your hero traits that readers don't like. Instead, give them weaknesses, but not things to dislike. Remember what I said about not giving your readers a reason to put your book down?

As I said earlier, a novel has a beginning, middle, and end.

The above beginning is not perfect. I'll never be a good enough writer to make it perfect. Before it's ready for submission, it needs to be rewritten several more times, and I'll point out a few of the mistakes as we go along.

Don't let rewriting frighten you. Seldom is a rewrite a "complete toss and start over." It's polishing. Was my transition smooth? Is there a better verb? Can one word replace two? Is the syntax correct? Are my characters engaging? Have I set the hook to keep the reader reading? These are some of the questions you'll know to ask when you finish reading this book, and you have to know the questions before you can search for the answers.

BACK TO PLOTTING:

The best texts on plotting are other well-written westerns or historicals or novels from the genre you wish to write. Study them. This is harder than it sounds. When I set out to study a good, well-written novel, I find that the story takes me into the trance all writers try to create, and I forget to look for the things I set out to study. It's easy to examine the bad books—you're not taken by the characters or the story. Concentrate on the good ones: they're the ones you want to learn from. Craig reads Louis L'Amour and Zane Grey to study prose to improve his science fiction because a well-told story crosses all genres.

It's easier to study the way the author did something after you've read the book once. The second time you're not so entranced by the prose or teased into turning the pages to see what's going to happen. Read it a second time, and a third, and look at it objectively.

What is the length of the novel? What are the lengths of the chapters? How many main characters did the novelist use? How many heroes? How many villains? Does the story have a theme? Is the pacing good? If he wrote in third person, did he switch POV? That is, did he see some scenes through the eyes of the hero and some through the eyes of the villain, or some through the eyes of minor characters?

These are plotting and construction—the hide, hair, and bones of a novel.

What's going to happen, when, and between whom? Through whose eyes is it seen?

If you are going to use multiple points of view, it's not important that you know before starting the novel whose point of view each scene is observed by. It will come to you as you begin writing that scene, and it's fairly easy to change and rewrite a scene if you decide it would be better through the eyes of another. Try to keep each scene in only one point of view.

SCENES:

Scenes? What's a scene?

Now that you have your idea of how long you want to make your chapters, and how long you think the story will be, and who your primary characters are, write in scenes. A scene is ***an action sequence containing conflict***. By action, I mean where something that moves the plot forward or shows characterization happens. It doesn't have to be a fist fight or a chase; it can be the hero having a conversation about going to the box social (a social during the 1900s) with the heroine.

Except for scenes that dramatically reveal characterization, there's a rule—the scene's primary ingredient is conflict. If it doesn't have conflict, it's not a scene and should be fixed or trashed.

Your heroine tells your hero she would prefer he didn't bid on her basket. He says it's a free world. Besides, she makes the best apple pie in town. That's conflict. Not the most exciting conflict, but it will make a scene. If they talk about going to the box social and there's no conflict, it's one sentence of another scene or a transition.

Ethan took Maggie's hand and told her he would see her at the social.

That's a narrative sentence out of a scene or a transition. This type of phrasing is used to stitch scenes together to deliver a chain of scenes, conflict, that lead the reader from start to finish.

How long is a scene? How long does it take? You can have one scene to a chapter or several scenes. You can break chapters in the middle of a scene (a Louis L'Amour trick). It makes for compelling reading because many readers put a novel down only when they've finished a chapter. It's hard to do in the middle of some kind of conflict—even if the chapter has ended. Louis L'Amour was a master of chapter endings and beginnings. He ended his chapters with a question many times, a question the reader wanted answered, so the reader read on. When the reader finished, he told his friend he couldn't put Louis's novel down.

One of the best writing tips I can give you, the one that will help make your writing more compelling, is to enter a scene late and leave a scene early. This is so important to good pacing that I'm going to set it out in bold print. If I could put it in hundred-point type, I would:

Enter late and leave early!

No one gives a damn if your characters greet each other! "Hello, how are you?" generally adds nothing to a scene. Neither does "goodbye." Enter the scene just before the conflict, or during the conflict, and leave the scene during or just after the conflict as a setup for the next conflict. Let me give you an example.

"Having chased the bat out the window, he pulled the covers up and went back to sleep." The end of a conflict, but tells the reader they can stop. We don't want the readers to stop reading.

"Having chased the bat out the window, he pulled the covers up and closed his eyes, but before he could go to sleep, a new noise made him shoot upright."

And keep charging forward. Doing something like that to end each scene forces readers to find out what is going to happen next. It's called an open loop, a sub-plot that is unresolved. Roll the open loops until you get to the end of the story. Close the last one and let the reader put your book down, unless you're writing in a series, then resolve the story of the book, but keep the overall series arc open.

That's my advice; charge forward, particularly for a first novel. Writing the novel will present you with those hard-to-anticipate questions we may have or may not have discussed. But you can't find the answers until you know the questions. Once you know the questions (which will raise their fuzzy little heads as *problems* when you write), you'll be able to find the answers.

HOOK:

Your first job is the beginning. Good beginnings have hooks. A hook is ***something that makes the reader want to keep reading (and if it has conflict, even better)***.

"It was the best of times, it was the worst of times..." We already showed the whole quote but it deserved a mention here. The dichotomy of good and bad. How could it be both? It opens the world before us where both best and worst exist simultaneously, depending on which social status one belongs to. "Let them eat cake." A great quote from a callous French princess. The worst of times.

Sidney Sheldon, one of the great masters, wrote (as my memory serves me), as his opening: *She wore a red nightgown so the blood wouldn't show.* Try to lay that little baby down without reading on. It would take a nuclear explosion to move most of us away from his novel.

The vignette began earlier:

The town and the saloon looked friendly enough. But looks deceive.

That infers that maybe they are friendly, and maybe they're not. *But looks deceive* is foreboding. Look out reader, trouble is coming.

Enough to keep you reading?

Tenkiller, my first western, begins:

Johnny Tenkiller got his name in the usual way, from his father. What was unusual was how seriously he took it. Talk was he'd killed ten men by the time he was twenty-one. But he must have lost count. He was still killing them.

That's a hook. Not the greatest. Not the worst. If it keeps the reader reading, it's a good one.

My second, *Mojave Showdown*, begins:

He watched with cold, dark, unflinching eyes.

Patience was the first thing the desert taught him and he'd learned well. He'd knelt unmoving, in the same spot, while the sun crossed a quarter of the morning sky and the roses and golds of the dawn turned to watery grays and washed out, wavering tans.

Who watched? What and why was he watching? Why did he stay stark still? Who was this man, taught by the desert? Do you want to keep reading? If you do, I succeeded. If not, it's a dismal failure; as dismal as watery grays and washed out, wavering tans.

One of my novels, a suspense, begins:

"Good God, Reno," he says, shaking his head as he reads. "In Manila, you killed a ninety-pound woman with a baby strapped to her chest. . . ."

"Good thing I wasn't paid by the pound," I mumble.

The hook is about telling the reader what the story is about without any detail. But you have to know why and how. Here is the opening to Craig's biggest selling series, the Terry Henry Walton Chronicles.

He came from the wasteland, broken and dying.

All he wanted was a drink.

But the old lady took him in, because he had kind eyes. She gave him water, food, and a bed.

Within a day, he started helping around the house. Then he straightened her yard, made things the way they were before.

Then the others came, not to ask but to take.

They didn't expect to find a man at her place.

Four arrived. The man walked out into the yard standing tall, giving the others a chance to leave. They didn't. With confidence, he walked into the middle of them and made them pay. He didn't kill them, only beat them mercilessly.

To send a message of "no more" to the other takers.

The old lady watched it all.

When it was over, she walked out to her porch and asked the man, "Why would you fight them like that?" She nodded to the rapidly disappearing group.

He answered over his shoulder, never taking his eyes from the retreating men. "Because you gave me water when I was thirsty, and you asked for nothing in return. As long as I live—" He turned to look her in the eye. "—I will be here for you."

"But I don't even know your name," she said.

"Terry Henry Walton, ma'am, but my friends call me TH," he replied.

"How many friends call you TH?" she pried.

"Counting you?" He reached up to wipe the sweat from his forehead. "That would be one."

Our (both Larry's and Craig's) books have sold well because the readers keep reading. We could tinker with them forever, but they were good-enough. Remember, the fans are the final arbiters. They've voted in favor of our books with their hard-earned money. It's our responsibility to give them the best we can in a reasonable amount of time.

THEME:

You've heard me speak of theme. Readers want your novel to have a theme—and so do you. Good triumphs over evil is probably the most common. You can't keep a good man down. A good woman is hard to find. As ye sow, so shall ye reap. Cheat me once, you're a fool; cheat me twice, I'm a fool. Themes. It helps you plot your novel if you have a theme. It helps you sell your novel if you have a theme. It helps drive you throughout the novel; it's the road map that gets you where you're going, to The End. Stay with it throughout the story, and prove it with what you write.

Think of three key points you want to carry throughout your story or series. Justice, humility, and a curious love of single malt whisky. Your readers will subconsciously attach themselves to these themes. Carry them through. Three is the magic number that readers can readily follow as they embrace them without effort. You may add tendrils, but never forget your tripod foundation.

And if you didn't get something right in your first draft? There's always the second draft. Clean it up and add what's missing. No one expects a perfect book from the first draft. And theme is that overall feeling you get from a book. It's good to go back through and make sure you achieved what you wanted to achieve with consistent application of the theme.

BACK TO THE BEGINNING:

One of the things you must do in the beginning of your novel—usually completed by the first fourth of the book and many times by the end of the first chapter—is pose the problem and define the players—the main characters. That is, if you want to write compelling fiction.

Ethan's problem is to get out of the mess he's in. The Union soldier who returns to find his sister kidnapped by the Crow has an obvious problem—find the girl. You also need to describe the setting and **the best way** is by dialogue and stage management. What people say and what they do can tell you a great deal about setting, time and place. It is the heart of characterization and doesn't slow down the story.

With contemptuous eyes the flat blue of the desert sky on a scorching day, the cackler slowly scanned Ethan. His mouth curled into a half smile, then with a whisper of metal on oiled leather, the Navy Colt appeared in his hand as if it had been there when he walked up. Ethan's mouth tasted copper fear. He could almost feel the lead slug tearing through his chest as his own gun cleared the holster.

The cackler's first shot, fired too quickly, cut the air near Ethan's ear like an angry hornet, and its muzzle blast slapped at him, stinging his cheek. As Ethan thumbed back the hammer, the boy's eyes flared in terror.

Ethan's carefully aimed shot took the boy square in the middle of his chest, blowing him off his feet and slamming him to the floor. The boy's flailing left arm knocked over a half-full spittoon. Tobacco juice and cigar butts mingled with the foamy blood pumping from the massive smoldering hole in his linsey-woolsey shirt.

Ethan unnecessarily thumbed back the Walker's hammer as the boy's second shot, more a death spasm, smashed one of the chimneys on the unlit coal oil fixture hanging high above him. Glass tinkled and fell; some floated on the growing pool of blood and spittle. The boy kicked twice, the Navy Colt slipping from his grasp, his eyes open, staring.

The room had reverberated with the echoing roar of the shots, but now was deathly still. Dust filtered down from the sculptured metal ceiling adding to the haze in the smoky room.

Ethan slowly panned the muzzle of the Walker. Did anyone else want to test his patient aim? No sound, save the boy's wheezing chest wound—then, with a last death rattle, it was still. The echo of Ethan's hammer ratcheting down was followed by the audible sighs of the poker players and the bartender.

Ethan sensed that more than just the gunfight was over. Something else, like a thorn finally removed from a festering sore, had ended in that saloon.

Taking his first breath since the cackler had grabbed for his gun, Ethan turned back and bellied up to the bar, then noticed that the boy's shot had scored a hit. His .44 slug centered a neat hole in the naked left breast of the reclining nude whose portrait hung, now slightly crooked, behind the bar.

The bartender jumped up, resting his ample belly on the bar, eyed the dead boy, and uttered a low whistle as if he was seeing something he didn't believe. Then he dismounted, turned, and carefully straightened the picture. Out of the corner of his eye, Ethan saw that the men at the poker table hadn't flinched, leaving their hands in plain sight on the green felt table top.

The bartender drew Ethan another beer, and the tension flowed out of the room as the beer flowed into the mug. The big-bellied man blew the foam off the top and set the mug on the bar.

"This one's on the house, but it better be your last." He gave Ethan a weary smile.

Without the cackling, it was pleasantly quiet.

Ethan holstered the Walker and upended the mug. The players divvied up the cackler's money and returned to their game.

Don't fall into the trap of doing it the lazy way, via narrative. *The sky was streaked with orange, the wind whipped.* That's not my way—not that many successful writers use that method.

Remember: pose the problem and define the characters.

CREATIVITY:

As it applies to writing—it's something we all do a lot of the time. It's wondering "what if." We have the initial idea for the scene, and then we have the ideas to make that scene better. How do you flesh out your work? Writers I know use all kinds of tricks like taking the dog for a walk, talking about it out loud with a disinterested spouse, telling your kids, bouncing it off another author. There is an endless number of ways to work through a scene. It starts with what if, and ends with, this makes sense.

As related to the vignette we started earlier with Ethan on the run, what would happen if Ethan's horse went lame? Would he trade his lame horse and his old Walker .44 for another horse?

Would you want a hero who'd steal a horse from an innocent rancher or farmer? And even if you did, would the market want a hero who would steal a horse?

Ethan notices from a rim rock on a high ridge that the posse has split up. One rider took a ridge on the left flank; one a ridge on the right flank.

How about Ethan taking one of the posse horses? Somehow, it's more acceptable to have Ethan trade his horse—even while he's discussing the matter with an unwilling man who's looking down the barrel of the old Walker. So we'll have him force a trade on a posse member who's part of Ethan's problem.

Or, what if Ethan slaps his horse on the rump and sends him on down the trail, thus throwing the posse off. Ethan circles back to the town on foot, goes to the livery, asks the old man running it where the cackler's horse is and steals it. Even more acceptable?

That's creativity, but creativity with the market in mind.

I will tell you that I read a wonderful western with a twisted dwarf as the protagonist. It's outside the norm, and I admire the author. He chose a tough path and made it work.

What if? That's creativity as it applies to writing.

Creativity is a product of the muse. So turn your muse loose.

MUSE:

If you study the craft of writing, and you must if you want to be a successful writer, you'll hear the term *muse*. The word is taken from Greek mythology. Muse was one of the nine daughters of Zeus who was said to reign or preside over the arts. She must have been a quiet, reflective girl.

My Random House dictionary defines the verb "to muse" as:

To think or meditate in silence.

A writing teacher will tell you to turn your muse loose. At times it's almost as hard for me to do it as it is to say it: Muse loose.

But you can do this anytime and anywhere. You don't have to have pencil and paper in hand and be sitting at your desk to be creating your story.

Where does a story come from in the first place? I'm asked that question dozens of times by people who don't write, but they're generally people who don't read.

The history of your own area? There are a thousand plots in the history of any town. Read the newspapers from the time known as the Wild West. Libraries have them on microfilm and reading old newspapers is not only fascinating and entertaining, but educational. And you get a wonderful sense of time and place.

After you read about a historical event say "*what if?*" What if, before the last railroad spike—a gold one—was to be driven at Promontory Point, they reached into its walnut box and found it missing (by the way, there were at least four spikes)? Your hero, the railroad detective, would be a little miffed, and his boss would be flat pissed. The beginning of a plot? A conflict? There is a historical piece of news and a creative change in the story that's the basis of a plot. A plot going to waste right under your nose right now.

But plots certainly don't have to be centered on historical fact, at least not a factual incident. Your plot is only limited by your ability to muse. Think creatively.

Say "*what if?*"

Creativity alone will not sell a novel. Your creative juices must be tempered with good sense. When you're first starting out, you may find that you have too many ideas. Control yourself and don't use them all in one book. Save some for the next story. Too much is just as bad as too little.

Your writing must have credibility in the sense that your characters must do what they do in a believable manner. And what they do must be in character, or you'll lose your reader. I'll say it again. Don't give your reader a reason to put your book down.

TIME AND PLACE:

Stropping a razor gives a sense of time and place. A bustle beneath a dress. A bone white water pitcher sitting in a bowl on a sideboard. A Seth Thomas clock ticking on the wall or being wound. The hiss of steam off a train engine. A sunbonnet. A cap and ball revolver. Buffalo. A space ship. A sail-driven ship. An outhouse or privy. Kennedy's assassination. Pancho Villa. Images flash in front of your mind's eye with each of those written words, and those images give you a sense of time and place.

A good western, historical, thriller, romance, or any other genre—check out Harry Potter if you disagree—has a continuous sense of time and place. The flavor of the feast you're going to lay before your readers is time and place. Reading other westerns and historicals will give you a sense of it and how to inject it painlessly into writing, but historical reading of nonfiction will give you the most accurate feeling for what it really is.

Every era, place, and profession has its own vernacular—words and expressions that are exclusive to time and place or endeavor. My Random House dictionary says, about vernacular, among other definitions:

...the native speech or language of a place. The language or vocabulary particular to a class or profession.

Using the proper vernacular for a time and place or profession is critical to giving the reader a sense of time and place. Immerse the reader.

How about this from The Man himself?

Out, out, brief candle!

Life's but a walking shadow,

A poor player that struts and frets his hour upon the stage, and then is heard no more:

It is a tale told by an idiot, full of sound and fury, signifying nothing.

Shakespeare flows differently from modern prose. In this

passage from Macbeth, the character is lamenting life but in a way that we wouldn't today.

Kat, years ago, wrote a medieval novel. A prodigious task, stepping back seven or eight hundred years in time. Talk about vernacular! It's not only the words used, but the sentence structure that's different from today's.

Newspapers, again, are a wonderful source of the flavor of the time. Not only do they tease you with plot material, but they tell you what the people in your story were talking about, how they were talking (pacing, vocabulary), what they were buying, what they were smoking and drinking, what those things cost, and on and on and on.

Another source is personal journals and diaries. Hundreds of journals were kept by people crossing the plains. They give you the flavor of everyday life. But you must remember that in newspapers, as well as most journals and diaries, there were things people of that time did not discuss. Rape, pregnancy, and sex were seldom, if ever, mentioned. But, we know they had sex then or most of us wouldn't be here.

Temper what you read using common sense.

I have a wonderful set of journals kept by Alfred Doten from 1849 through 1903. The publisher of these journals (University of Nevada Press) has taken a good deal of time to reconstruct the erasures—Doten married and took great pains to erase all references to his visits to the bawdy houses in Virginia City, among other incidents that make for interesting, and factual, reading.

Great dictionaries are available, giving you the jargon of a particular endeavor—the mining industry, the cattle industry, the logging industry, gambling. My friend Bob Burton has written a dictionary on spy terms: *Top Secret: A Clandestine Operator's Glossary of Terms.* It's invaluable if you're writing a spy novel or thriller set around the many sub-rosa organizations.

I collect reference books of many kinds and get a great deal of pleasure from reading them, even when I'm not looking for a particular phrase or word. I have mystery and romance dictionaries on the shelves. I fear I'm addicted to vernacular works of all kinds.

And, of course, any period book will have words utilized in that particular period.

I also rent old movies. When writing about a particular period or profession, some of the old movies offer great vernacular.

The trick is to get those things into your western or historical or romance in a way that educates the reader and entertains him. Time and place without his knowing.

Give him the medicine with a dose of syrup.

The jingling of big roweled Spanish spurs and the echoing of footfalls on the mud, smashed egg shell, and broken-crock-covered floor announced his entry.

That's time and place and a better way of letting the reader know Ethan what big Spanish roweled spurs are rather than saying: Ethan dismounted. He wore a broad brimmed Palo Alto hat, homespun britches, heeled boots, and big Spanish roweled spurs. He walked across the board walk and entered the saloon, pushing aside the batwing doors. His spurs jingled as he walked. The floor was covered with mud, broken egg shells, and broken crocks.

His flailing left arm knocked over a half-full spittoon, and tobacco juice and cigar butts mingled with the foamy blood pumping from the massive hole in the boy's linsey-woolsey shirt.

Let me tell you, pardner, there ain't many half-full spittoons or linsey-woolsey shirts around the bars I frequent today. There sure as hell ain't any nickel beers. That's time and place.

Writing details—time and place—into your western or historical, or even your contemporary, is a necessary labor.

By introducing time and place the way it was done in the vignette, you not only accomplish the introduction and inform the reader, but you've moved him into the saloon (called "stage management" in novels). You've gotten another sense into your writing (the reader can hear the jingling of those spurs). And you've given the reader the feel of the saloon. It's obviously not the Ritz. Somewhere else in the scene you can introduce more time and place. Feed it to the reader sparingly because maybe they are seeing them for the first time. Take them on a learning journey with giving them a laundry list of strange and foreign words. And for those comfortable with the vernacular, they'll read quickly through it. In both cases, you don't want to give the reader a reason to put the book down.

I expect it won't take long to figure out where this next scene takes place.

A young woman wearing a fashionable spacesuit approached. Terry wasn't sure whether it was armored. He resigned himself to the fact that she was new, like her spacesuit. She approached, offering her hand.

"My name is Rivka Anoa, and I'll be working with you on your franchise contract for All Guns Blazing. Do you have any questions before we start?"

"We'd like to see the All Guns Blazing before anything else.

Are you old enough to go in there? You look pretty young," Terry told her.

"So do you," Rivka deftly replied. She was shorter than Char by half a head, with blonde hair, hazel eyes, and pale skin. "I'm twenty-five, I'll have you know."

"I'm not twenty-five, and I'd like to see what I'm going to spend Nathan's money on," Char said.

"What are you, thirty-five? That's not that big a difference."

"I think I'll be..." Terry stopped and started counting, ticking off his fingers as he went. "Round it up to one ninety. You know what that means! Somebody is going to hit the big two-oh-oh this year."

"Why?" Char rolled her eyes and groaned. "Why did you have to bring that up?"

"Because I need to throw you a surprise party," Terry replied nonchalantly.

Char turned to Rivka. "Which way to the bar? I could use a drink."

"Follow me, please." She winked at Char before shielding her mouth from Terry Henry. "I can get a wheelchair for the old guy if you'd like. I know you're not a year over twenty-nine. You look magnificent! I love your eyes."

Char loved the infectious exuberance of youth. "Lead on, Queen's Barrister. Wherever you go, we shall follow—as long as you're going to All Guns Blazing. If you're not, we'll find our own way."

They took an elevator to the promenade level, where Rivka held the doors for them to exit.

"This looks the same," Char said.

"All Guns Blazing is a brand new addition to Onyx Station.

One of the signature elements is the seven by twenty-meter window looking into space. It is made using proprietary technology that will be part of the contract. The beer vats and brewing system must be purchased through The Bad Company. There is no proprietary technology there—it's just beer—but the style of vats is unique and trademarked by AGB Enterprises."

"Stop right there, barrister." Terry crossed his arms, puffed up his chest, and pushed out his biceps. "It's never just beer... There's an AGB Enterprises?"

That's from Judge, Jury, & Executioner Book 1 by Craig Martelle and Michael Anderle.

SENSES:

Taste, touch, smell, sound, and sight?

As you write, you need to pull your reader into the trance of the story if you want your novel to be compelling. All of us are sensual; some more than others. Some are stimulated more by one sense than another. All writers appeal to sight in their writing—unless writing in the first person from a blind person's POV. Some writers appeal to taste, touch, smell, and sound. Great novels appeal to all the senses.

Mopping the sweat from his brow with the back of his hand, Ethan glanced at the afternoon sky. Indian summer; still no sign of storm.

A sense of touch and sight.

The trail-tough cowhand rubbed the black whisker stubble on his chin with a knotted callused hand. "That'll do," Ethan said, and laid a nickel on the rough plank.

A horse fly buzzed around, inspecting the coin, as Ethan waited.

Rubbed the stubble. A knotted callused hand. The rough plank. A horse fly buzzed. Touch, texture, and sound. Senses. Also, a nickel for a beer is a *sense* of time and place. The fifth dimension. Not only do my favorite bars not have spittoons, I'm again sorry to say, they don't have nickel beers.

The room reeked of dust, sweat-soaked men, and cigar smoke.

Sense of taste.

Ethan's mouth tasted copper fear. He could almost feel the lead slug ripping through his chest as his own gun cleared the holster.

Taste and touch again. It is also internalizing. As I reread this, I see an edit, which I'll leave in and point out to you even though it's embarrassing. The word *mouth* should be eliminated. Of course he tasted it in his mouth. How the hell else do you "taste." *Ethan tasted copper fear* is correct.

Get the senses all in, and your writing will be better for it. Read Kathryn Lynn Davis's work, particularly *Child of Awe*, for great writing using all the senses.

Another example from Nomad Redeemed by Craig Martelle and Michael Anderle.

"Absolutely not!" he answered. "But I will get you one if you like?"

"What? That is the most foul concoction I have ever smelled. I can't imagine putting any of it in my mouth." Her face contorted with the thought of the smell, which made him want one even worse.

He excused himself to go outside and pull one of his precious jars from the shaded crawl space of the house. It was cool enough outside that it was almost like drinking a cold beer, except for the fact that it was still too warm and Char was right. It was really foul-tasting.

But there had been no other beer for a lifetime. He wondered if he was mis-remembering the taste.

Nope. It was bad.

He unscrewed the lid and sniffed. The mash was too heavy. Cut the recipe in half or double the water, maybe prime it with a touch of cherry juice or something before bottling. He was a fan of man-law that declared no fruit in beer, but twenty years after the fall of civilization, maybe the law was outdated. He brought his beer inside, sipping it slowly, trying not to gag, while making a show of smacking his lips and saying, "Ahhh."

Clyde wouldn't even drink the beer, and Terry had seen his dog eat a rat that had been dead for a week.

REWRITING:

This brings me to a good spot to discuss rewriting. I mention it now because one of the things I do when I rewrite is make sure I've gotten all the senses in. I also work on my verbs. (Notice I changed tearing to ripping.)

Ethan tasted copper fear. He could almost feel the lead slug tearing through his chest, as his own gun cleared the holster.

That was the first way I wrote it.

Ethan tasted copper fear. He could almost feel the lead slug ripping through his chest as his own gun cleared the holster.

Ripping seemed a stronger image to me. A thesaurus is a wonderful tool. Use it. You want the verb that gives you the clearest and most concise image of what you want to portray.

I also dropped the comma after chest. Commas slow your writing, and in rewriting I seldom find myself adding a comma. I delete twenty-five commas for every one I add.

It has been said, by writers far more knowledgeable than I, that writing is rewriting.

Writing is rewriting.

So important, so basic to the writer, so necessary to good writing, that I set it alone and bold in the text. A writer who claims he writes his work only once is writing only for himself. Don't be concerned when you read what you've written and it stinks. Write it again. And again. And again. Sometimes you'll get a sentence right the first time; most often not. Even if it's right the first time, maybe it's not the best way to do it.

I've found if I leave a "perfectly polished" piece for two weeks, then go back to it, I find ways to improve it. Sometimes I can't believe how bad that "perfectly polished" piece was.

But there comes a time when you must submit it. Do your best. Then mail it away. It won't sell sitting around waiting for another rewrite.

Every time I pick up one of my published novels, I gag, knowing I could have written it better. But I submitted it, thinking it was the best I could do at the time, and keeping within a time constraint, usually a manuscript delivery date. But you always think you can do better, and in my case, I usually can.

This is an important point. Do the best you can but don't belabor perfection. There is no such thing as perfect. The readers determine if they want to keep reading. If they do and they're hungry for your next novel, that's what perfect looks like. Also, you can't get better if you keep rewriting the same sentences. Declare victory and move on to the next book. The readers will tell you if you did a good job. Your copyeditor could provide feedback as well so you write the next book just a little bit better. Practicing is learning.

Mickey Spillane said it best with the first chapter sells this book and the last chapter sells the next.

There comes a time, however, when you had better say "enough is enough" and submit it.

CHARACTER TRAITS:

As in life, you want your characters to be different. Tall, short, fat, thin, jovial, morose, but each a character unto himself. My faithful dictionary defines character as:

The aggregate of features or traits that form the individual nature of some person or thing.

The key here is *individual nature.* Ethan may swagger while the cackler struts. Habits, looks, actions, reactions, likes and dislikes, speech and laughter, and so much more are the ingredients that make each of us different from our fellow human beings. Your characters should portray the same differences. Like time and place, these character traits should be given to the reader in small doses and subtly so that he comes to like or dislike your character as he would if he met him on the street. Those who form fair opinions about people usually take some time to do so. First impressions aren't always the right ones. Give your characters some time to impress the reader with their individual personalities. You have a lifetime of experiences upon which to draw. What do people do who you like? What are things that draw your eye and ear? Work those into your characters.

When I say write what you know, this is what I mean. Turn your life experience of human interaction to develop your characters.

Ethan dismounted and loosened the cinch so the lathered roan could catch its breath. Mopping the sweat from his brow with the back of his hand, he glanced at the afternoon sky. Indian summer, still no sign of a storm. But it would come. Digging a handful of grain out of a saddlebag, he offered it in his palm. The big roan mouthed it as Ethan scratched the horse's ears with his free hand.

You get one kind of impression about Ethan from the above few lines. What if we'd written:

Ethan dismounted and pulled the cinch tighter. The roan had been acting up the last few miles. It would serve the knot-head right to stand with a binding cinch while Ethan got a beer. Hell, Ethan hadn't eaten or wet his throat either. The horse could wait.

Does that give you a different opinion of Ethan's character? How?

The trail-tough cowhand rubbed the black whisker stubble on his chin with a knotted callused hand. "That'll do."

The above lines give you one impression. What if we'd written:

The cowboy looked from side to side, shifting his eyes as he spoke, not looking at the bartender. "I'll bet the beer's flat," he mumbled so low the bartender had to lean forward to hear.

Or:

The cowboy rubbed the soft blond fuzz on his chin. "That sounds real fine. You know, I haven't had a beer since the last time I was in St. Louis. I've got an aunt in St. Louis. Larapin' fine lady. Why, I remember one time. . . ."

Another impression?

Character is what's done and said by your players. Keep their character consistent. That's not to say that your good guy should be all good or your bad guy should be all bad. Few people are all one or the other.

Character can be shown by what your player thinks.

Remember, if you write in the first person, you can get inside the head of that first person narrator, but no one else's. If a character says what he thinks, you're getting inside his head via dialogue.

If you write third person omni, you can get inside the head of any of your characters to see what they think, merely by going there.

What a character thinks when you internalize, or when he says what he thinks in dialogue, or what others think or say about him helps the readers form an opinion of him. That's not to say if one of your characters calls another a drifter and a bum, that he is. If the reader knows the character of the accuser, sometimes his opinion is the last the reader will believe.

Just like real life.

What he looks like, what his habits are, what he thinks, says, and does—or doesn't say and doesn't do—establishes character.

INTERNALIZATION:

For a character to internalize, the reader needs to know

what he's thinking and how he feels. This doesn't mean you have to write:

Ethan looked across the room. A man who'd been scalped and had his nose cut off sat drinking a beer. His head was a mass of scars. Ethan caught his eye. I'd hate to look like that ol' boy, Ethan thought, staring. Ethan immediately regretted his reaction as the man caught his gaze and dropped his gaze to his beer.

It would be as effective, maybe more so, to write:

Ethan looked across the room and caught the eye of a man who'd been scalped and had his nose cut off. His head was a mass of scars. Ethan winced, then regretted the action as the man lowered his eyes and stared into his beer.

In the first instance, we wrote, *Ethan thought*. In the second, we wrote *Ethan winced.*

We know Ethan winced because he hated looking at the man with the terrible scars. We know what he thought, because of how he reacted. This is internalization via characterization and through it we get to know Ethan.

If we had said:

Ethan looked across the room and caught the eye of a man who'd been scalped and had his nose cut off. "Why, look at that." Ethan pointed. "If that's not the by-God ugliest man I ever seen, I'll dance an Irish jig right here on this bar." The man cut his eyes down at his beer.

Another impression of Ethan?

Ethan tasted copper fear. He could almost feel the lead slug ripping through his chest as his own gun cleared the holster.

We didn't say: Ethan was afraid. We said he tasted fear; he could feel the slug tearing through his chest. That's internalization; we don't specifically say what Ethan thinks. We show it.

If you want your readers to get involved with your characters and your story, you must let them get to know your characters. Internalization is one major way to accomplish that—in small doses given with the sugar of action. Compelling characters in conflict make a compelling read. If we don't know the characters well, or don't want to, then we don't care about what happens to them, or about reading on.

A great internalization trick is the following.

"Are you coming to the box social?" she asked.

"I don't know," Ethan said, allowing his glance to drift down across the ruffled bodice of her dress. It would take the whole damn Sioux tribe to keep me away, he thought.

"Well, I'll have a basket if you're going to bid." She flashed a coy smile, turned and walked away.

"Probably won't make it," Ethan called after her, his hand in his pocket fumbling with the three dollars he had left to his name. She flashed the smile over her shoulder, then disappeared around the corner of the mercantile.

I wonder if I can sell my saddle, Ethan thought, and headed for the livery.

He says one thing, but means another. Some things can only be done via internalization.

POV TO POV:

There are all kinds of transitions in the novel. Transitions of time, transitions of place. One of the most important and difficult, at least for me, is knowing when and how to change POV. It can confuse the reader if you do it incorrectly. Worse, it can make your story difficult to read without the reader knowing why.

In the example, most of the time we stayed in Ethan's POV, but we also went into the bartender's POV for a moment.

...the bartender gave the dusty stranger a tight smile. "Beer?"

Ethan could see the bartender give him a tight smile. But would Ethan think of himself as "the dusty stranger?" That's a slight change in POV and would probably have been better if written: *...the bartender gave Ethan a tight smile.* We know that Ethan is a stranger in that saloon and no one but Ethan knows who Ethan is.

The trail-tough cowhand rubbed the black whisker stubble on his chin with a knotted, callused hand.

That's also a change in POV The bartender would be thinking: This ol' boy is a trail-tough cowhand, and look at that black stubble on his chin. Ethan probably would not think of himself as a trail tough cowhand. And it's hard to see your own chin. Granted, he would know his beard was black and, by rubbing it, he would know there's a stubble. The point is that POV is difficult, but mastering it will make your writing flow, and readers buy.

Let's do the whole thing over, first definitely staying in Ethan's POV, then making a transition into the bartender's.

From across the rough plank bar, the bartender gave Ethan a tight smile. "Beer?"

Ethan rubbed his chin with a knotted callused hand. "That'll do," he said, and set a nickel on the bar.

Max, the bartender, turned and drew the beer. I wish these saddle tramps would stay out of here, he thought, clamping his jaw. The bum should have used his money to buy himself a shave. Max set the beer in front of the man and snatched up the nickel. Then he went back to shining his bar glasses.

As Ethan took a deep draw, he heard shrill drunken laughter....

That's a POV transition. We went from Ethan's POV to Max's POV then back to Ethan's.

When and how often to switch? Some great writers switch many times; some seldom. A switch like the above one is not particularly good because it makes the reader work. The less you make the reader work, the better chance you have to keep him in the spell and not lose him. Unless it's important to the reader to know the bartender thinks Ethan is a saddle tramp and a bum, you've gained nothing.

TRANSITIONS:

The other basic transitions are from time to time and from place to place, or both—from one place and time to a later or earlier time (an earlier time would be a flashback) and another place.

Ethan backed out of the bar through the batwing doors, then spun and in two long strides pulled the lead rope from the rail and mounted the roan. The street lay deep in shadow, and a few merchants were shuttering their windows and doors to close up.

By the time Ethan crossed the Laramie, it was full dark and the roan was heavily lathered. Hours later, when he reached the Medicine Bow, the roan was winded and the sky (at his back) was beginning to gray. Still, Ethan couldn't take a break. After crossing, he dismounted for the fourth time during the lone night's ride and walked to give the horse a blow.

A transition of both time and place.

Sometimes a double drop is necessary to give emphasis to a transition:

The street lay deep in shadow. A few merchants were shuttering their windows and doors to close up. Ethan restrained the gelding, who wanted to run, but no more than he had to restrain himself from galloping out of town.

(a blank line here is a double drop)

Big John Albertson stood staring down at his dead son. "The bastard what did this will pay," he muttered, then looked up. "The man that shoots the murdering scum down like the cur he is and hangs him up for crow bait will receive a month's wages."

That's a double drop—just an extra line. It's a visual break in the text. Some writers use:

These asterisks can be implemented with a double double drop to show a definite transition. I use both the double drop and the above. Others use decorative line breaks. Software such as Vellum can make anything look spectacular. Whatever you use, the copyeditor might change it if it is vague or misleading, so the real question is "Is it clear?"

Ethan spurred the roan into the shallow Laramie. He was bone tired and the horse's plodding pace caused him to doze. The shallow river reminded him of Cross Creek, back home. His father used to take him fishing on Cross Creek.

"You dig the worms, boy, and I'll break us a willow pole," Henry Estler would say, winking at his son. Ethan would run for the shovel.

"Papa, I bet I catch the biggest," Ethan challenged.

"I'll bet you do, son," his father said.

We changed time and place inside the paragraph, and we effected a flashback. The trick is to use a word or two in the past tense, then go right on as if you're there.

"You dig the worms, boy and I'll break us a willow pole," Henry Estler would say, winking at his son. Ethan would run for the shovel.

That phrase managed to transport us back fifteen or twenty years with a simple "would say" and "would run," and transport us to a place near Cross Creek.

"I'll bet I catch the biggest," Ethan challenged.

Notice we didn't say "had challenged." We went to present tense within the dialogue and past as the story is written in past tense. Suddenly but smoothly we're there with both in one sentence.

It also managed to tell us Ethan's last name. A piece of information fed with a little action.

Also it gave us a little more insight into Ethan's character and his father's.

It was a transition and a flashback inside a paragraph. That flashback story could go on and on if you needed to establish Ethan's character, or his father's, or their motivation. It would be called a back story and it's not commonly used in westerns, but occasionally in historicals. My advice is to stay away from it, at least in your westerns or short romances. Charge forward with your story, and let what your characters say and do establish their character.

A common complaint from readers is that writers don't use enough transitions and don't make them clear enough. If it breaks the reader's concentration and he has to go back in the text to see how he got to the Medicine Bow from the saloon, you've broken the trance. Don't give anyone an excuse to set your novel down!

ACTION:

Here's an action scene from one of my crime novels *G5, GEE WHIZ*, remember that one of the rules of a good crime or thriller novel is deeper and deeper in trouble. To set this scene up, our heroes have just escaped from recovering a fifty-million-dollar business jet from a small South American country while they've escaped in a small, but very fast and effective, two-seater amphibious aircraft. The pilot, call sign Wetback, has taken a round and is wounded. This is a single event that takes place over a few seconds. It should read quickly.

"The bleeding seems to have slowed," I say, encouraged.

"Yeah, that's the good news. The bad is I'm flying over the fucking jungle with somebody who's made about five landings on a wide swatch of airport, and there ain't no wide swatch of airport around."

I don't bother to respond, then I'm over the lights of what appears to be an estancia or maybe a mine or timber company headquarters. If there's an airstrip, I sure as hell don't see it, but they wouldn't have it lit unless they were expecting a plane. I see Madman fumbling for the radio mike, then get it to his lips. "Mayday, mayday. Anyone on the radio."

Silence as I circle.

"Mayday," he says again, and to my surprise a voice comes back.

"Si, señor. Problema?"

"Yeah, we got a problem. We're out of fuel. Can you get some lights on your strip?"

"You English."

"American."

"You got helicopter?"

"No, airplane."

"We got no strip, only helicopter pad."

"Fuck."

"Señor, we is a Catholic facility."

"Sorry. We're turning our lights on so you'll know where we're gonna crash."

"We will watch, señor."

He turns to me. "Any sign of any kind of clearing?"

"I'm gonna parachute—"

"You've got a fucking parachute. Only one I guess?"

Even under the circumstance, I have to laugh.

"Madman, the airplane has a parachute. An emergency chute. I'm taking her up," and just as I get it out, the engine coughs, and I doubt if I'm taking her any higher than she already is. I check the altimeter. "We've got nine hundred meters. Is that enough?"

"How the fuck should I know. My F16 didn't have a chute. It had an ejection seat."

"Guess. And tell me what to do."

"It doesn't matter what I think. It is what it is. You got the chute release control?"

"It's a lever overhead between the seats."

"Make sure it's operable, then cut the throttle."

I don't have to as it runs completely out of fuel. Suddenly there's a very ominous dead silence...and I hope the "dead" part is not foretelling.

"Okay," he says, thinking I cut the engine. "Ease the stick back and just as she shudders about to stall, as slow as you're gonna get, pop the chute."

"Remind me never to get in a fucking airplane again," I say, as the plane slows and I do as instructed, easing the stick back.

"You probably won't have to worry about making that decision," he says, as the stall warning light flares on the control panel and the warning buzzer goes off like a cheap alarm clock.

"Yeah, probably," I concur, loud enough to be heard over the angry buzzing.

The plane starts to nose over and I pull the lever, having no idea what's going to happen, as we begin to accelerate toward the ground.

I hear a swooshing noise and it sounds like the flapping of fabric, then feel a violent jerk and we're suddenly fairly level again, but swinging as if on a pendulum.

"Crocodiles," Madman says.

"Crocodiles?" I ask.

"Yeah, fucking crocs, or pythons, or man eating fucking jaguars, or some fucking thing has to be waiting for us, the way it's been going."

"You're a glass half empty kind of guy, aren't you?"

"I'm a fucking realist."

"We're still descending at three hundred meters a minute." And I said she'd float like a butterfly, but she's falling a little like a rock.

"Crap," Madman says, then adds, "I hope what's waiting is a soft landing. That's too fast."

"I hope what's waiting for us is a bottle of Jack Daniels...."

"The blood of Christ."

"Pardon me."

"The sacrament is probably the only booze they have at some Catholic facility."

"That'll do," I say, and then something crashes, banging my head hard on the windscreen, and suddenly we're upside down hanging on our seatbelts, bouncing back and forth like we're the pinball in an arcade machine. Then we jerk so hard I about lose my molars and the seatbelt bites deep into my gut.

We're canted at a forty-five degree angle, with the seats still under us, but at least we've stopped.

"We're alive," Madman says, with a little astonishment.

There's a small bug-out bag behind the seats, and I dig into it and come up with a flashlight. Push the cowling up, and shine it out to see we're obviously in a tree with the chute entangled in the branches above. Hallelujah. And we seem to be fixed in place. Then I shine it down and to my dismay, the light diminishes before ground appears. I have no friggin' idea how high we are in this bloody tree. The trunk is only ten feet to my right, and appears to be about two feet in diameter. I know that many of these big jungle beauties, and there are millions of acres of them, are as big as four feet at the base, so we could be a hundred feet in the air—ten friggin' stories.

"Don't step out for a smoke," I suggest.

"Long first step?" he asks.

"Longer than the beam of the flashlight."

"I guess we wait for morning."

"I have to get to a phone."

"Try your cell."

I laugh. "It isn't that big a facility."

"Now who's a half empty glass kind of guy?"

To my great surprise, Wetback is not nearly as stupid as he looks. I am. For I get a signal and, in moments, am talking with a bail bondsman buddy, Fast Freddy Franklin, who I've worked for in Florida, and he is happy to make points with the DEA, for whom his brother-in-law, Irish Jack O'brien works, by informing them that the repairman and friends are delivering a couple of tons of grade A cocaine to them via a beautiful G5 and, in a few hours, they'll be making a soft touchdown and welcoming them aboard. I spent many an hour with Freddy chasing down skips and even broke bread with his brother-in-law more than once. A good guy, for a fed.

Now if only Wetback and Skip don't decide to fly away to a profitable locale and become multimillionaires comfortable on some island retreat. But I know Skip wouldn't do that.

My second call is to Carmen. She must have been sitting on the phone as she answers before the first ring's complete. "Ola," she says, and sound anxious.

"Ola, senorita."

"Are you okay, the news channel and the Internet is buzzing about a raid on our Air Force headquarters...."

"Attributed to whom?" I ask.

"So far it's Sendero Luninoso or Shining Path...no mention of a bunch of gringos."

"Any mention of a couple of tons of cocaine?"

"Cocaine...at the Air Force headquarters?"

"Yes, a couple of tons."

Writing action is a special talent and one you must master if you're going to write western adventure novels, thrillers, mysteries, or any novel that involves action.

Remember how we talked about pacing earlier? That was in regard to pacing throughout the whole book. In an action scene, pacing is *everything*. And I don't mean pacing as it relates to the book as a whole, but rather as it relates to a single scene.

Not only is pacing important, but verbs are critical. Some words evoke an image of immediacy. Active voice keeps the action flowing. Passive jerks your action to a halt.

Ethan's carefully aimed shot took the boy square in the middle of the chest, blowing him off his feet, slamming him to the floor.

...something crashes, banging my head hard on the windscreen, and suddenly we're upside down hanging on our seatbelts, bouncing back and fourth like we're the pin ball in an arcade machine. Then we jerk so hard I about lose my molars and the seatbelt bites deep into my gut.

Would you have gotten the same image if I'd written "knocking him to the floor" or "hurling him to the floor?" I doubt it. I'm sure there are better verbs than "carefully aimed." Carefully aimed slows the action down too much for my taste. How about "Ethan's steady shot?" Or "Ethan's studied shot?" They don't seem to slow the action quite as much as "carefully aimed." And "bites deep into my gut" is a pretty visual image and you can feel it. We've all been bitten.

Action is usually written in short paragraphs. Choppy, quick, with verbs that connote speed.

Upon musing, the above might have been better written:

Ethan's shot slammed the boy to the floor. In the middle of his chest, the linsey-woolsey shirt turned red.

Why? We know if he's slammed to the floor, he's blown off his feet. Yeah! We've ferreted out a redundancy. We've avoided slogging through the sludge of a badly thought out sentence.

That's cutting and editing.

One of the mistakes beginning writers make in action is leaving it! What I mean is:

Ethan quieted the roan with the tail of the reins and glanced over his shoulder to see the twenty-man posse at full gallop a quarter mile behind. The roan stumbled, tried to regain his balance, but went down. Flying over the horse's head, Ethan lit on his back, winded. But he held onto the reins.

He'd been thrown a hundred times before, when he had a piebald horse who was always stumbling, so he knew how to land. That piebald was a great animal, but a clumsy sonofabitch.

The posse crossed the ravine, a hundred yards away and bearing down.

As Ethan remounted, he noticed puffs of smoke from the muzzles of the pursuers' guns.

Being shot at wasn't new either. One time down on the Brazos, a band of Comanches had run him and the piebald for most of twenty miles.

Lead buzzed over his head like wasps on the warpath. Ethan again used the tail of the reins on the roan.

What's wrong with that? Plenty of action and we got a little background information and characterization in.

Wrong! Get background and characterization in when you're not trying to involve the reader in the immediacy of the action.

Try this instead:

Ethan quirked the roan with the tail of the reins and glanced over his shoulder to see the twenty-man posse at full gallop a quarter mile behind. The roan stumbled, tried to regain his balance, but went down. Flying over the horse's head, Ethan lit on his back, winded. But he held onto the reins.

The posse crossed the ravine a hundred yards away and was bearing down.

As Ethan remounted, he noticed puffs of smoke from the muzzles of the pursuers' revolvers. Lead buzzed over his head like wasps on the warpath and again he used the tail of the reins on the roan.

Stay with the action. Don't distract the reader. Move forward. Don't flash back, even for a second, when writing action scenes. Breaking into the action only irritates the reader, who's relishing the action sequence. For many readers, it's the reason they've put up with your campfire, information, and characterization scenes. Don't slip into passive voice, either. Keep it active and vary the sentence length toward the shorter end as that allows the reader to go quickly, increase the heart-beat, keep the action vibrant.

And be sure to use strong action verbs. Read James Reno, a master of western action verbs. I don't think anyone ever walked anywhere in a Reno novel. He charged, lumbered, stomped, sauntered, strolled, marched, ambled, shuffled, pranced, etc.

Action is drama at its finest. And drama is compelling. And compelling reading is what sells readers—on your writing.

BREVITY:

Now is a good time to talk about brevity. Make every word

count. (Which also, by the way, is the title of a great book on writing by Gary Provost.)

Here's a classic example, given in writing classes:

For sale, baby crib, never used.

Think about it.

A diamond of lean writing that evokes images.

Another example—would it be better to say:

Ethan climbed up on the horse or Ethan mounted the horse?

The proper, most efficient, verb is the son of brevity.

Ethan looked at the scarred man and wondered what had happened to him.

Or:

Ethan studied the scarred man.

Look for the right word. Your reader will get more information with the action and will stick with you. Your writing will be compelling.

The interior of the saloon seemed plebeian.

Is that the right word? Not unless you want Ethan to come across in a way where the author is trying to sound smarter than your reader.

If the proper verb is the son of brevity, Jacqueline the Ripper is the daughter.

The room shook and reverberated with the echoing loud roar of the three shots, then lay deathly still. Dust hazed the lighting and filtered down from the sculptured metal ceiling adding to the haze in the smelly, smoky room.

Isn't shook and reverberated the same thing? Rip it out of there. Cut. Use the best verb.

Isn't loud and roar the same thing? Cut.

The dust hazed the lighting and filtered. Isn't it close enough to the same that it's redundant? Rip it out. Hazed created haze? Why?

Smelly! Smoky! Didn't we say it before? Slice it to the bone in your best Jack the Ripper imitation.

The room reverberated with the roar of the three shots, then lay deathly still. Dust filtered down from the sculptured metal ceiling, adding to the haze in the room.

Not Hemingway, but better than the first version.

Stay away from the disease *redundancy* as if it were the black plague. Redundancy makes work for the reader and for the editor.

Like all of us, editors don't like to work any more than they have to.

The classic comment about brevity in writing came from the great western and mystery writer, Elmore Leonard, who said, "I try to leave out the parts people don't read."

SENTENCE VARIETY:

Sentence structure can become boring. Reading, even if done for pleasure, can become tiring—and quickly—with bad writing.

The town and the saloon looked friendly enough but looks deceive.

Ethan dismounted and loosened the cinch. The horse stood quietly and caught his breath. Ethan mopped the sweat from his brow with the back of his hand. He glanced at the afternoon sky. Still no sign of a storm. It was Indian summer. There was nary a drizzle of rain but it would come.

Ethan offered the roan a handful of grain he'd dug out of the saddlebag. The big roan mouthed it as Ethan scratched the horse's ears with his free hand. He listened for sounds from inside the Laramie Queen. A cool beer would suit him fine. He needed to resupply at the mercantile. He only had three dollars left. Then he had to ride out of town to camp on the banks of the Laramie. Tomorrow he would make the banks of the Medicine Bow.

Boring, boring, boring. Subject, verb, subject, verb. Same length sentences. Puke! Reader rejection before they finish the first page.

Kat is a master of sentence variety and a great editor. She was editing my last contribution to our joint effort, *Tin Angel*, and found that every other sentence in an action sequence I'd written began with "As." Watch for repetition in your writing in any form. Unless it's there for a specific reason, rewrite to give variety. I probably would have found it on rewrite, but with a good editor at hand, I got lazy.

Needless to say, Jacqueline the Ripper went to work and I was returned a hen-scratched section for rewrite.

Your writing should be like music. It has rhythm, but it also has the tinkling variety of melody.

The town and the saloon looked friendly enough. But looks deceive.

Ethan dismounted and loosened the cinch so the lathered horse could catch its breath. Mopping sweat from his brow with the back of his hand, Ethan glanced at the afternoon sky. Indian summer, still no sign of a storm. But it would come. Digging a handful of grain out of a saddlebag, he offered it in his palm. The big roan mouthed it as Ethan scratched the horse's ears with his free hand. All the while, he listened for sounds from inside the Laramie Queen.

A cool beer would suit him, before he resupplied at the mercantile with his last three dollars then rode out of the town to camp alone on the banks of the Laramie River. With luck and easy country, tomorrow he would make the banks of the Medicine Bow.

It's not Beethoven or Mantovani or Willie Nelson, but it's better than the first example, and the reader won't throw it aside without reading the next page.

Sentences should vary in length and in construction.

Ethan dismounted and loosened the cinch so the big horse could catch its breath.

Dismounting, Ethan loosened the cinch so the big horse could catch its breath.

The big horse caught its breath after Ethan dismounted and loosened the cinch.

Ethan dismounted and loosened the cinch. The big horse caught its breath.

There are lots of ways to say the same thing. Make sure your sentences vary in length and construction.

EMPHASIS:

The placement of the subject of your sentence will clue the reader as to what you, the writer, feel is most important.

Ethan checked the .44 in his holster, strode noisily across the boardwalk and entered the dingy saloon.

Is Ethan entering the saloon the most important segment of the sentence?

Ethan entered the dingy saloon, striding noisily across the boardwalk while checking his .44.

Is Ethan's action in checking the .44 the most important segment of the sentence?

Ethan entered the dingy saloon after checking his .44, striding noisily across the boardwalk.

Is Ethan's noisy striding the most important segment of the sentence? In the last instance, the reader will believe so.

John F. Kennedy was shot and killed in Dallas on November 22, 1963.

On November 22, 1963, in Dallas, John F. Kennedy was shot and killed.

John F. Kennedy was shot and killed on November 22, 1963 in Dallas.

If I were writing about November 22, the first sentence would work best, if about Dallas, the last. If I were writing about Kennedy's assassination, the middle sentence is the better one.

The segment you want to place the emphasis upon, the segment you think is the most important, should end the sentence. Keep the reader focused on what's important.

DIALOGUE:

Poorly written dialogue often is the first clue that someone is reading a new writer's work.

If there's one tip to writing good dialogue, it's reading it aloud. If it's difficult to say, it's tough to read. If it's tough to read, it slows the reader down, and it's not compelling.

You've seen some great examples above of dialogue in action. How many tags did you see? Were they distracting or did they keep you reading?

Remember to keep dialogue in character. One character may talk one way, a different character may talk another. The words they use, the contractions, and the pacing, all tend to characterize the speaker.

Dialect is an easy way to characterize, but unless it's extremely well done, it slows the reader down. Often, heavy dialect can be used when a character is first introduced, then can be severely curtailed as you proceed. Use only a key phrase, like "Ye" instead of "You" as you go forward, and your reader will still recognize the speaker.

"Aye, boy. I rounded the horn before ye blessed this earth," the old marinero said.

"What brought you here?" the boy asked.

"Same as ye, the gold."

"And have you found it?" the boy asked, eyeing him.

"Have ye?"

The use of a continuing "ye" tells you who the speaker is. Most readers are not fond of dialect. Take great care with it in your first novel, as you may spend an inordinate amount of time trying to get the dialect correct and losing the story. The story is king! Dialogue supports the character development while also moving the story along. Do not let it derail your flow.

And remember, most importantly, dialogue is people speaking. Listen to people talking if you are interested in writing good dialogue—and you had better be, if you want to sell your work. People don't always answer questions asked of them. People don't always finish sentences. Just two clues for good dialogue.

Listen with a writer's ear to people talking.

In my opinion, Robert Parker was the best in the biz at writing dialogue. Read him, check out the white space in his books. You don't need to belabor description or characterization if your dialogue covers it well.

Remember the old rule, "writers are allowed to stare." That means watch and listen to other people as they talk, and see how conversations/interactions actually work.

DIALOGUE TAGS:

He said, she said, John said, Marsha said, he said vindictively, she said shyly. These are tags.

A simple 'he said' or "she said,' 'John said' or 'Marsha said' is a popular way to tag a speaker. It disappears to the reader's eye. He doesn't even realize he's reading it, so it doesn't interfere with the trance.

Obviously, you don't use *John said* continually. The next time he speaks, particularly if he's talking to a woman (and he's the only male in the room) *he said* is sufficient. If it's perfectly clear he's the one who's speaking, no tag is even better. The same goes if you get too creative with dialogue tags. Too many variations of tags is just as distracting as *always* using said and asked.

Read it back and make sure there's no doubt about who the *he* is in *he said.* If there's a doubt, make it *John said* or give John an action after the statement.

"Don't go in there." John smiled, waiting to see the effect of his warning.

The use of an adverb in a tag—he said vindictively—makes

the reader work harder. A simple *he said* is read unconsciously. If your dialogue was smooth and your scene properly portrayed, the reader should already know the character was being vindictive.

In well-written dialogue you can often drop the tag lines altogether.

"Aye, boy. I rounded the horn before ye blessed this earth," the old marinero said.

"What brought you here?" the boy asked.

"Same as ye, the gold."

"And have you found it?"

"Have ye?"

Another thing to watch for:

"Not yet," the boy smiled.

That's wrong. You can't smile a statement.

"Not yet," the boy said, smiling.

Or,

"Not yet." The boy smiled.

That's one of the ways to get the smile in.

Some writers are effective at putting the tags in front.

Smiling, the boy answered, "Not yet."

I just read a whole novel with the tags in front. He was a brilliant writer. More often it's distracting. You can try it, but for your first novel, maybe it's best to do it the conventional way.

CRUTCH WORDS:

When you're editing your own work, there are danger signs to watch for. The most obvious of these are lazy words. 'Was', 'very', 'that', and others really don't add to your writing.

Ethan was galloping up the hill. The posse gained and was very close behind.

Or:

Ethan spurred the roan, clattering up the hill. Chips stung his face as the granite beside his head splattered with a ricocheting shot.

'Was' can be a lazy word. 'Ethan clattered' is a much better visual image than 'Ethan was galloping'. Even 'Ethan galloped' is better than 'Ethan was galloping'.

Ethan was very tired.

That's telling.

Ethan collapsed.

That's showing Ethan's exhaustion, and it's a much, much better way.

When you use WAS it shouts out to you: "YOU HAD BETTER TAKE A HARD LOOK AT TENSE AND VERB!"

Ethan thought that he should mount up and ride before the posse that followed crossed the ravine.

Or:

Ethan thought he should mount up and ride before the posse crossed the ravine.

If I had saved all the "that's" that I have taken from my writing, I would have a room that's full of them. OOPS! What I should have said was: If I'd saved all the "that's" taken from my writing, I'd have a roomful.

See what I mean?

ACTIVE OR PASSIVE?:

Another time "was" is an indicator that your writing is weak is when it tells you you've fallen into the passive voice.

The article was written by Frank.

Frank was given a huge advance by Wonderful Publishing.

The novel was written about his life.

Or:

Frank wrote the article.

Wonderful Publishing gave Frank a huge advance.

He wrote about his life.

The first set of sentences is passive and the second is active. Active, as you can see, is usually livelier and shorter (remember brevity). It's also more direct.

If you want your writing to be hard-hitting, write in the active voice. Writing soon becomes boring and tedious in the passive voice.

AUTHOR INTRUSION:

Any time you let the reader know he's reading, you break the spell of good writing. The object of good writing is to put the reader in the scene. You want him to finish the scene covered with sweat, or with a knot of fear in his stomach, or with an audible sigh of relief. When you, as author, intrude—when you yell at him "I'm a writer, and you're reading my stuff," you break that spell.

The town and the saloon looked friendly enough. But looks deceive.

"But looks deceive," touches on author intrusion. Why? Because we are not in POV yet. If we had introduced the scene:

Ethan drew rein on the roan and gazed up at the false front of the Laramie Queen. The town and the saloon looked friendly enough, but looks deceive.

It's always better to be in POV, so the reader doesn't think the author is injecting his opinion into the story.

Clichés are a form of author intrusion. My trusty Random House dictionary (if I keep writing "trusty Random House," it will become a cliché) says:

A trite stereotyped expression; a sentence or phrase, usually expressing a popular or common thought or idea that has lost originality, ingenuity, and impact by long overuse, as *sadder but wiser* or *stronger than an ox.*

Don't use clichés. They take away from your writing and distract the reader—unless, of course, you want to characterize a character by having HIM use clichés.

The cackler's first shot, fired too quickly, cut the air near Ethan's ear like an angry hornet. The muzzle blast slapped at him, stinging his cheek.

Like an angry hornet? That gives the reader an image but is it the right one? And has it been used so many times that it's lost its impact?

The cackler's shot cut the air near Ethan's ear and its muzzle blast slapped at him, stinging his cheek.

Jacqueline the Ripper did a little more than take out the cliché, and it's a better sentence and image for the cut—and more compelling.

Foreboding, if it's done incorrectly, can also be author intrusion.

Ethan sat on the rise overlooking Coppertown. When he'd entered the Laramie saloon, he had no way of knowing the kill-

crazy youth awaited him—or that in Coppertown, it would be worse.

That's classic author intrusion. Clancy has been guilty of it, Grisham has been guilty of it. You're not in Ethan's POV, for Ethan has no way of knowing that in the next town it will be worse. There's a much better way to do it, staying in POV:

Ethan sat on the rise overlooking Coppertown. He hesitated, unsure if he should spur the roan—a niggling sensation gnawing at him, a sensation he knew he should listen to. But his scorched mesquite bean coffee and the last of his jerky mocked him.

And growling stomach overcame whispering caution.

Hoisting his .44 an inch, he reined the roan down the slope.

That's foreboding, but in POV. Something inside Ethan is telling him that he shouldn't ride into this town. Not the author telling the reader that Ethan shouldn't ride into Coppertown.

Another comment on author intrusion. I just finished reading a great book by a *New York Times* bestselling author. Early on in the novel, he wrote a good scene, then closed with, "but he wouldn't discover that until later." That is author intrusion at its worst. It's a jarring change of POV from a character—where it should be—to the author who's not, or shouldn't be, a part of the story. Don't tell the reader that you're a writer telling them a story. It sandwiches a level between them and the characters you want them to become involved with, an unneeded level that continues to interfere with the reader's trance.

MOTIVATION:

It's critical that you give your characters proper motivation.

The fact that Ethan and the cackler had a run-in on the Lazy Z ranch gave credibility to the gunfight in the saloon.

Most people aren't devil-mean or angel-good but rather something in between. Readers like the worst villains to have redeeming qualities and the best heroes to have flaws.

But whatever good qualities or flaws they have, make sure they have motivation to act as they do.

If Ethan had merely slapped the cackler and disarmed him, would he ride out of town at a gallop and would the posse come after him? Have proper motivation for what happens in the plot.

DRIVING LINE:

The single most important thing you have in plot is the driving line through the novel. The driving line is very close to theme, but not quite the same. The driving line is usually ***the protagonist's goal***, and that is not necessarily the same as the theme. His desperate attempt to cross Death Valley in order to reach the California gold fields can be the driving line to the theme, *persevere and you will succeed.*

Ethan escapes town and runs for his life—*his survival is his driving line.*

The Union soldier on a quest to find his kidnapped sister —*driving line.*

Shane has made a vow never to pick up his guns again —*driving line.*

Edward Fitzgerald Beale wants to open up the West, and a wagon road will do it—*driving line.*

Find the driving line, stay with it, and your novel will be compelling.

STYLE:

Style is simply ***the way you write***. As a beginning writer, don't worry about style. You will develop style. Style is what identifies our writing, even without our name attached to it. You don't have to see the book's title to know that Hemingway wrote the story, not after you've already read a couple of his books.

Don't worry about style; it will come. Don't try to copy some great writer's style. If you do, you'll never develop your own.

And I didn't say don't *study* it. Just don't *copy* it. When studying style, look for the phraseology that grips you. The words. The sentence flow. All those things that keep you reading. Remember that the goal is to make your story one that a reader cannot put down.

MAKE 'EM LAUGH?:

Sure. As long as it's part of the plot and not an overwhelming part—unless you're writing a comedy. Like humor, sorrow should work into the plot. A genre western reader picks a western off the rack because he likes adventure and the old West. If he wanted a good cry, he'd reach for something else. In a historical, you can do what you want. And again, the above rules were made to be broken.

In a romance, it's make 'em laugh, make 'em cry, make 'em wait, and turn 'em on. Those same ingredients, with turn 'em on meaning with action as opposed to sex, make a good western. Like romance readers, western readers expect you to be faithful to the genre. Don't make humor or sorrow your primary plot device.

Humor worked for *Blazing Saddles*, but Mel Brooks was not one to be constrained by convention.

MAKE 'EM CRY?:

You bet. Ask James Waller and his all-time best-selling *Bridges of Madison County*. Like making them laugh, making them cry takes a special talent. Much of it, I believe, is pacing. Kat has a special talent for writing emotion into her novels, and romance lends itself to emotional reads. Study other writers' pacing to determine how they made you cry, then try it in your own writing. Making the reader cry is the ultimate in reader involvement, even more so than making the reader laugh. And believe me, readers remember it, and you, if you involve them to that degree.

And there are writers' tricks to doing it—I've never had a reader tell me they cried when reading one of my passages about a character of mine dying, except when it was a horse. Kill an innocent, if you want them to cry, but only an innocent about whom they care. If the person is a nobody to the story, the impact will be exactly that. I'd suggest using the death of a beloved character sparingly. We know that it worked for G.R.R. Martin, but it is a rare thing when it works. I wouldn't bet my publishing career on the chance that I could regularly kill my main characters without readers abandoning ship.

Another adage is that if the author isn't crying while writing it, the reader isn't going to cry while reading it.

WORD COUNT:

Here's the old-school typewriter method. Count every space (character and space) in a maximum line on the page (I use sixty) times the number of lines on the page (I use twenty-five) and divide by six. In the format I use for novels, this results in two hundred fifty words to the page. Even though (due to white space and half pages at beginning and end of chapters) the words aren't there, count them.

Now, use your computer's word counting feature. Every word-processing program has one. For example, in Microsoft Word, at the lower left corner of the page, you'll find the page count (based on the page size and layout you've selected) and the word count. You need do nothing special, just look and see where you are. As of this moment, Write Compelling Fiction is exactly 46,650 words. Apple's Notes, Scrivener, Google Docs, all the programs have the word count feature.

The word count gives you an idea of how long your eBook might be. We have a number of books around 60,000 words, and Amazon credits us about 300 pages. Maintain consistent formatting, and if your page count seems too low, then contact Amazon and ask for a review.

The digital page count matters less on other retailers, but is still important when marketing because some readers want as much book as they can get for the price. Paying to have a paperback made is dependent upon page count, too. The more pages, the higher the cost if you self-publish and use the print-on-demand option.

THE MIDDLE:

As I mentioned before, all novels have a beginning, middle, and end.

The most important thing to remember about the middle of your western or historical or any other novel you write, is not to let it get middle-aged. As with many middle-aged folks, the middle gets saggy.

Don't allow your novel to get a saggy middle. Things must continue to happen to your hero; he must get deeper and deeper into trouble, only to escape, then fall deeper again. With proper pacing, your plot will not suffer from a saggy middle.

On the open road, truckers riding the middle of the convoy would call it "in the rocking chair." In a book, the middle doesn't mean that you can sit back and cruise, letting the beginning and ending carry the story. The middle needs to be just as engaging, always moving the story along. Adding conflict, resolving conflict, creating more conflict, but moving toward the big showdown at the end.

In the movie, Tombstone with Kurt Russell, the famous shootout at the OK Corral was in the middle, maybe even toward the front of the movie. The good guys won! Wait, things just took a turn for the worse. Then deeper. The good guys hit bottom and came back with a vengeance, clawing their way through an army of bad guys. One by one.

THE ENDING:

The most important thing to remember about the ending is to wrap it up—all of it. Remember the posse member Ethan traded horses with? Somewhere in the novel we should see the posse member limping back into town, leading Ethan's lame roan. Otherwise, we'll wonder about him, and the ending won't truly be an ending.

Your ending can be happy or sad, or somewhere in between, but it must answer all the questions posed within the novel, resolving all the issues unless it's part of a series, then you'll want to leave issues unresolved that carry from book to book (that is, the series arc).

The Union soldier finds his sister and brings her back with him, or, to his surprise, decides to honor her wishes. She'll be better off with the Indians since she and her half-breed son will be ostracized if taken back to town.

The ending can be a lot of things, but it must resolve the issues.

Nearly all of Craig's novels are what he calls escape fiction. They give the reader a quick escape from the troubles of the day, immersing them in a story with vibrant characters that the reader can relate to. Even in one of Craig's long series, he still wraps up the story within each book. The stories build on each other for the overall series arc, but the reader gets a high when the protagonist, our heroes, win by the end.

In one series, Craig wrote a tragedy into the second last scene of book fourteen. It picked up a little with the last chapter, giving the reader hope for the next book. Craig estimates that he lost nearly fifty percent of his readership on that series at that point because of making his readers feel bad. Half his readers did not pick up book fifteen. At least not right away. With the release of books sixteen and seventeen, some of the readers came back, but it was a significant hit right to the pocketbook. Delivering on reader expectations is critical. Craig thinks that if he had added another chapter or two, it would have delivered the high that readers needed to crave the next book.

But none of it's worth a damn if you don't write it accurately.

FIRST TIMERS:

A note to first time authors! The most important thing you can do in regard to selling your work is to finish your book. The hardest thing you'll ever do is write a book. And until you've written it, you can't address everything else that needs to happen to sell it.

Finish It!

Don't be misled that you can sell your fiction work from an outline or a partial submission as a first novelist. How many people have you heard say "I'm going to write a novel." The difference between saying it and doing it is months of hard work. Family and friends will be skeptical and respond to the above statement with a "Sure you are." Most of them won't know someone who has written a book.

A complete novel is the first-time novelist's proof that he or she can finish a full-length work—it's indisputable. And the fact they've started on their second is encouraging to readers who become fans and are looking for more.

Don't wait to hear from the agents or publishing houses to begin your second novel. If you're a writer, write. Besides, it fills the time and keeps you from brooding about the fact that you haven't received a fat advance check in the mail. And it proves to a potential reader of your first novel that you are serious about writing and will continue to produce.

And there's no sense in publishing an unfinished work. All you'll do is anger readers, unless you do something weird such as asking them how they'd like to see it end.

Get off your duff and finish the damn thing.

Then decide – send an email to legacy publishers or give self-publishing a try. After all, you have a finished manuscript that should be earning you money. Don't squander that opportunity. Check out Become a Successful Indie Author by Craig Martelle. It'll tell you all the steps you need to take if you want to publish. Demystifying the process for new and experienced writers alike.

"When I was a little boy, they called me a liar, but now that I'm grown up, they call me a writer."

Isaac Bashevis Singer: Writer

6

THE FINAL ARBITER

The people willing to pay for your work are the ones you should listen to. Whether they are readers or acquisition editors throwing fat royalty advances at you, everyone else is a far second in the value of their opinion.

But you should listen to us!

We believe you should because we've listened to our readers, and that's what we're sharing with you.

Don't get wrapped around the axle with people who don't read your genre. My mother hasn't read any of my science fiction. My dad reads all my books even though they aren't his genre. I hope my grandkids some day pick up my stories and like them.

Many people don't read their reviews because sometimes the criticism can be harsh. The internet is a great place because we can work from anywhere and sell our books from the comfort of our own homes. The internet can also be a dark, troll infested labyrinth. Trolls are a sign that you've arrived. You have to be able to separate the artist from the business. If you rely too much on your ego, you will have problems when the boo-birds come calling. All professional athletes deal with it.

Are you any less professional as an author? We say "No!" Once you are making money and hopefully earning your living from your words, then you are a professional. Practice and make yourself better. Professional athletes have coaches. An author has fans. I turned some fans into my insider team, my coaches, so to speak.

They were appropriately critical, but with the intent to make me better, not make themselves sound smarter than me. We had a shared purpose based on mutual respect, and it made my stories that much better. Improvement, but in a way that the readers liked.

I didn't change because other authors told me to change. I took what I had and made it better. My fans told me that. They like my old stuff, but they like my new stuff, too. The stories are sound, but I'd like to think that my style is better. Fewer repetitive words. Crutch words. I'm getting pretty good now at not using them in the first place.

My (Craig) latest release has topped the charts and garnered some incredible reviews. These are what matter to me and show that I've done my job. Thirty reviews in less than a week and twenty-nine of them were five stars. Here are some examples.

"Yet another book in a great series. Thoughtful but with action to keep things moving. Witty but not overbearing or forced. Characters are well developed and flow together."

"In contrast to prior volumes in the series, *Fratricide* has less battle action and more courtroom drama that is actually gripping and thought-provoking. Rivka's newly-assigned super-frigate has promise of holding its own in future space battles, yet compelling character interactions, many quite humorous, continue to charm without massive mayhem scenes. Our author, Craig Martelle, skillfully paces the narrative and sustains reader focus.

"*Fratricide* is highly recommended recreational reading. The story exceeded my expectations and provides some practical life lessons as a bonus."

"An exceptional story detailing an enigmatic definition of life! An emotionally charged look defining what constitutes a living entity! A must read for any Sci enthusiast!"

"I'm reading all of Craig Martelle's books in this series. It's extremely hard to find such an interesting and exciting author who not only writes intelligently but also provides top rated plots, characters and excitement in the stories. I've enjoyed all of his books so far and look forward to when his new ones are released."

They are the final arbiters. They vote with their money.

Don't get me wrong. I went through a lot of pain and anguish with my editors who taught me much in crafting sound sentences and better paragraphs. The fans have responded and appreciate those efforts. It's also less expensive to edit a book that's written cleanly. I save money by sending my editor a draft with few errors.

You can read self-help books like this one to help you visualize the many things you need to keep in mind while writing your books. You can review these books to see if there's something missing. Practice what you learn by writing. Reading alone won't help you be a better writer. Reading and writing together will put you at the top of your game.

And then when you are publishing with regularity, you can listen to your fans, your insider team, and your other readers. They may try to lead you astray by asking you to write something that isn't in your wheelhouse or something that won't sell. Avoid getting pulled down a rabbit hole.

Stay true to yourself and the greatest bulk of your fans.

Don't let the stray one-star review get you down. They happen. I think I have 75 one-star reviews (as of when I wrote this). I also have 4291 five-star reviews. I read the one-stars. Most of them are by people who are angry at life. I can't fix that, but I can keep writing for the people who like my stuff, all 5000 of those who took the time to leave a review and the hundreds of thousands who have bought my books.

This is a great ride if you listen and learn. Over one hundred books later, I can't imagine being anything other than a writer.

7

EXAMPLE TEXTS

As promised at the beginning, here are improved copies of a couple chapters, one from Larry and one from Craig. Writing is reading, but the story is printed only in your mind until you transfer it to paper.

TROUBLE IS A HUNTER

By
L.J. Martin

L. J. Martin
1234 Happy Lane
Bakersfield, California 93389
(805) 555-1212
(if you're agented, use their info here)

Chapter One

The town and saloon looked friendly enough, but looks deceive.

Ethan dismounted and loosened the cinch so the lathered roan could catch its breath. Mopping the sweat from his brow with the back of his hand, he glanced at the afternoon sky. Indian summer, still no sign of storm.

But it would come.

Digging a handful of grain out of a saddlebag, he offered it in his palm. The big roan mouthed it as Ethan scratched the horse's ears with his free hand. All the while, he listened for sounds from inside the Laramie Queen. A cool beer would suit him. One beer, then he'd resupply at the mercantile with his last three dollars, ride out alone, and camp on the banks of the Laramie River.

With luck and easy country, tomorrow he would make the banks of the Medicine Bow.

But luck hadn't been exactly doggin' his trail for the last thousand miles. Ethan had been gnawing on venison jerky and drinking trail coffee, the drover's curse, made from scorched stone-smashed mesquite beans for two weeks. Some real grub would suit him fine.

But trouble wouldn't suit him, and trouble had a way of dogging his trail.

No sound came from inside, so Ethan tied the roan to the hitching post near a wooden water trough and watched as the big horse muzzled aside some floating green moss and drank deeply. Ethan hoisted his heavy old Walker Colt's .44 an inch, making sure it rode free and easy in its holster. With his broad-brimmed Palo Alto hat he knocked the dust from his breeches and chaps and it billowed into the air.

The jingle of his big roweled Spanish spurs and the echo of his footfalls announced his entry as he shouldered through the batwing doors. Across a floor littered with smashed egg shells, broken crocks, and mud from the rutted street outside, he made his way to the rough plank bar. The room reeked of dust, sweating men, and cigar smoke.

From a few feet away, the bartender gave him a tight smile. "Beer?"

Ethan rubbed the black whisker stubble on his chin with a knotted callused hand. "That'll do." He slapped a nickel on the rough wood. A horse-fly buzzed around, inspecting the coin, as Ethan waited.

The bartender dipped the beer from a keg then set the mug in front of him. Without comment, he snatched up the nickel and strode away.

Backhanding the foam from his handlebar mustache, Ethan cut his eyes. In the rear of the saloon, four men sat playing poker under a wafting cloud of cigar smoke. One of them cackled a grating laugh. The cackler was the bantam rooster who—with five riders to back him up—forced Ethan to backtrack twenty miles and ride around the Lazy Z.

Ethan sighed. Suddenly the beer didn't taste so good, He'd seen the like of the boy in a hundred towns. All mouth and spit, no grit. He wondered if the men the boy played cards with were Lazy Z riders. No, he decided. One looked like a drummer, the other two were probably merchants.

"You're not from around here?" the bartender asked.

"Nope." Ethan turned his attention to the big man whose belly kept him some distance from the bar he mopped with a rag.

"Where you from?"

"Yonder." Ethan motioned with his head as he answered.

"Never heard of no town named 'Yonder.'" One side of the bartender's mouth curled up in a half grin.

"You must work on the local newspaper," Ethan said, returning the half smile, which tilted his mustache to a slant.

The man's look hardened. "Just makin' conversation."

"Well, look at that." The cackler's voice rang from the rear of the saloon. Ethan heard the footfalls of the approaching cowhand, but chose to ignore him.

But he wouldn't be ignored.

He bellied up to the bar next to Ethan.

"Gimme a shot of Mr. Noble's finest, Barney." The cowhand slapped the bar with the flat of his hand. As the bartender poured him a shot from a bottle he kept under the bar, the cackler turned to face Ethan.

"Ain't you the saddle tramp who tried to cross the Lazy Z?"

Ethan stared straight across the bar. He sipped his beer and backhanded the foam away.

The boy's voice dropped to a harsh whisper. "I'm talking to you, saddle tramp."

Ethan didn't respond.

The cowhand cackled. "This ol' boy must be deaf as a stone, Barney."

Ethan could feel the hair rise on the back of his neck. Slowly, he turned to face the mouthy youngster. "If you're talkin' to me, boy, the name is Estler...Mr. Estler. And yes, I'm the rider who was crossing the Lazy Z. I appreciated your fine hospitality."

"I don't much like your tone, saddle tramp."

Caution gave way to studied anger. "Careful, pup, you don't have a half-dozen drovers backin' you up this time."

The men playing poker stilled and the bartender backed away as the boy stepped back, his hands held out from his sides, his stance inviting trouble.

"I don't need help from any man, and you call me pup again, you'll have to prove it."

Ethan turned back to the bar. "Another beer, Barney."

"You yella' too, saddle tramp?"

"Walk away," Ethan said quietly, staring straight ahead.

"Good idea," the bartender quietly added.

"Shut up, Barney. You wanna prove I'm a pup, saddle tramp?"

Ethan slowly turned to face the youth. "You're proven' it by courtin' trouble, son. And you're about to get a portion too big for a guppy to swallow."

With contemptuous eyes, the flat blue of the desert sky on a scorching day, the cackler slowly scanned Ethan. His mouth curled into an arrogant smile, then with a whisper of metal on oiled leather the Navy Colt appeared in his hand as if it had been there when he walked up.

The bartender ducked below the bar.

Ethan tasted copper fear—a taste that cut his wolf loose.

He could almost feel the whelp's lead slug ripping through his chest as his own Walker cleared the holster.

The cackler's first shot—fired too quickly—cut the air near Ethan's ear and its muzzle blast slapped at him, stinging his cheek. As Ethan thumbed back the hammer, the boy's eyes flared in terror.

Ethan's studied shot took the boy square in the middle of the chest, slamming him to the floor. His flailing left arm knocked over a half-full spittoon. Tobacco juice and cigar butts mingled with the foamy blood pumping from the massive hole in the boy's linsey-woolsey shirt.

Ethan unnecessarily thumbed back the hammer as the boy's second shot smashed one of the chimneys on the unlit coal oil fixture hanging above him. Fine shards of glass rained over the boy, some floating on the growing pool of thick blood and spittle.

The boy kicked twice, the Navy Colt slipping from his grasp, his eyes open, staring.

The room had reverberated with the roar of the shots, but now seemed deathly still. Dust motes filtered down from the sculptured metal ceiling, adding to the smoky haze. The bartender rose tentatively, wide eyed.

Ethan slowly panned the muzzle of the Walker. Did anyone else want to test his patient aim? No sound, save the boy's wheezing chest wound—then, with a last death rattle, it stilled.

Ethan's hammer ratcheting down echoed across the saloon—and was followed by the audible relief sighs of the poker players and the bartender.

Ethan sensed that more than the gunfight was over. Something else, like a thorn finally removed from a festering sore, had ended in that saloon.

Taking his first breath since the cackler had hoisted his Colt, Ethan turned back and bellied up to the bar. With a grim look, he noticed the boy's shot had scored a hit. His .44 slug centered a neat hole in the naked left breast of the reclining nude whose portrait hung, now slightly crooked, behind the bar. The bartender jumped up, resting his ample belly on the bar so he could see over it, eyed the boy on the floor, and uttered a low whistle as if he was seeing something he didn't quite believe—then he bellied back off the bar, turned and carefully straightened the picture.

Out of the corner of his eye, Ethan saw that the men at the poker table hadn't flinched, their hands still in plain sight on the green felt table top.

The bartender drew Ethan another beer, and the tension flowed out of the room as the beer gurgled into the mug. Ethan blew the foam off and set the mug on the bar.

"This one's on the house," the bartender said, "but it better be your last in this town if you know what's good for you." He flashed Ethan a weary smile. "That boy's daddy will be comin' to find you, and he'll be on the prod."

"For his sake, he'd better shoot straighter than his whelp."

"That 'whelp' was the fastest gun in this town. His daddy's not so fast, but he won't come alone. And most of his boys ride for the brand."

"I guess I was lucky not knowing this pup was 'the fastest gun in town.' It mighta throwed my aim off."

The bartender managed a nervous smile.

Without the cackling, it was pleasantly quiet.

Ethan upended his mug. The players divvied up the cackler's money and returned to their game.

Ethan eyed the boy. He'd been wrong about the kid, he had too much grit for his own good. He looked from the boy to the poker players, then to the door.

"Guess I best be moseyin' on."

"That'd be best for you. I'll tell the sheriff he drew down on you first, if that's a comfort to you. O'course the sheriff is the boy's cousin."

"You do that, Barney," Ethan said. Tipping his hat to the bartender, he made for the batwings, keeping an eye on the bartender and the players. It wouldn't do to be back-shot, even by a smiling man.

"Won't matter a hoot nor a holler to his pa," Ethan heard the bartender say as the batwing doors closed behind him.

Trouble is a hunter, Ethan thought as he mounted the roan and urged him into a brisk walk. Passing several men who were running for the saloon, he spurred the roan into a distance-eating lope...

THE GREEN DOOR OF FATE

By

Craig Martelle

Chapter 1

"In our obscurity – in all this vastness – there is no hint that help will come from elsewhere to save us from ourselves. It is up to us." **Carl Sagan**

Dig Site, Sagittarius Major, on the eastern edge of the Fermi Desert, southern hemisphere

A door unlike any other door…

"Why are we here?" the foreman droned. His crew leaned on their shovels. A Green Door set into the bedrock of the substrate. Fossilized but not. There was no going through it.

It simply was, and it was not. Maybe it was Schrödinger's door.

Doctor Somal laughed lightly to himself before waving at the workers. "Put them away. We'll call you when we're ready to dig."

"You'll call and schedule. I'm not your slave. We have plenty of other work," the foreman declared, making a face and slashing his hand at his crew. "Pack it up!"

With newfound vigor, the crew collected their gear and, with a spring in their step, hiked away, following their foreman's lead.

"That was disappointing," the professor's aide said softly.

The small woman, shy on the best of days, watched them go. Now more comfortable in their absence, she straightened her shoulders before turning to the Green Door and staring in silence.

"Seven days, and we have learned nothing," the professor stated as if attempting to shame the door into giving him an answer. Or at least offer a clue.

"If you would indulge me, please," the aide started, "why did they put someone with a Ph.D. in philosophy in charge of the Green Door Project?"

Somal had hired her because of her impeccable curriculum vitae but had spent almost no time getting to know her before their arrival at the dig site.

"Why, indeed?" The professor was in no mood to answer the question. Not right then. He needed to think about what would happen after having nothing to show for a week's work. How much time did he have before he would be called to answer?

A deliverable, they had told him. They needed a deliverable.

He had only questions.

The Glory Star, Clarion, Sagittarius

The bar where most of the outpost's management decisions were made. People spent too much time there. And money. Way too much. Many complained that there was jack-all to do on Sagittarius Major.

And many complained just to complain. It had evolved into an art form all its own.

The patrons came from all walks of life. Farmers and

workers made up the vast majority of settlers. The planet was known for its nutritionally rich bio-matter, which was launched to orbit, where it would freeze, then be consolidated and exported quarterly in massive freighters. Other workers became space ranchers, wrangling the loads from floating space buoys into container netting before strapping those to the freighters' superstructure. Little more than a network of girders and beams, space's supply chain took advantage of the lack of gravity, the vacuum, and the extreme cold to optimize shipments.

And profits.

The Glory Star. Birthplace of the best and worst rumors, and the place they were resuscitated after the truth had killed them and perpetuated until something better took their place.

But the worst never died. Like a maleficent religion, they dug their claws into a human brain and never let go.

"Aliens!" the man declared, his calloused hands constantly in motion. Dark ale flecked his beard, and spittle flew from his mouth.

"No schlock, it's aliens. A door solid within the rock? It's a billion years old, I heard."

"A billion!" The bearded man's eyes shot wide in wonder. He looked out the window at the gray sky beyond. "Looks like a drencher's coming."

"What's new?" His compatriot appeared to be a professional cubicle dweller—an office worker with clean hands, his eyes darting randomly around the Star. But looks meant nothing. He was in the dive with everyone else, doing what they were doing.

Gossiping.

The office worker stirred the chum to draw out the sharks.

"I thought there'd be more visitors sucking off the government teat."

"Who wants any of those contractors out here? Stupid! This is a whole bucket of stupid wrapped inside a nice warm moron blanket." The farmer pounded his fist on the bar for emphasis before adding, "Another round for my friend and me."

The bartender held out his hand. The farmer waved his credit chip close enough for the soft ping to register payment for the drinks before the man started mixing them. A gin sour fizzy for the well-dressed nob. A stout beer for the farmer.

The two clinked glasses before getting down to the serious business of bad-mouthing governments and their representatives, both near and far.

Earth Central, Secretary-General Binlow Dietrich

A modern office, loaded with technology and conveniences, all turned off. The Secretary-General didn't trust any of it. He leaned back in his chair and looked at printed pictures of the Green Door, an object that carried its own classified code-word. But the real word had already gotten out.

Too many space settlers, unsophisticated souls running their mouths.

He shrugged, his internal conversation found no fault with the general populace of Sagittarius Major. No one kept secrets anymore. That was why the technology in his office was for show, not use. That was why he guarded every word.

His assistant knocked politely on the door.

"Yes?" he said softly. His assistant had uncanny hearing. He wondered if she was disseminating tidbits she had heard through the door. He had no evidence, but he remained wary.

As a professional politician, he had political enemies on all sides. He was their natural target since he had what they desired.

The position of ultimate power. He had been them. Once.

It had all changed ten minutes after he took the seat. *Wanting* and *having* are two far different states of being. He was aging more quickly than other men of his years.

Having was nothing like wanting.

From his office, the view of Geneva was magnificent—the best in the city. He didn't get to enjoy it. He would look out and try to contemplate what the lives of the billions in his charge should be like, but the seat of power was disconnected from the vast majority of humanity, so much so that he didn't remember who the common person was. Citizens of Earth. Nations, countries, city-states, protectorates, commonwealths, and more. Unified Humanity. The UH didn't get into individual governments' business as long as they paid their dues. Some paid more, and all received.

And that was the source of his pain.

He leaned back as a stout, petite woman opened the door.

"Your two PM is here. Secretary Anderson from the United States."

Binlow plastered a false smile on his face. "Send her in! I always look forward to her visits."

He didn't.

The Secretary-General walked around to the front of his desk, where the tradition of sitting next to her would continue. He didn't use the furniture as a barrier against any of his guests. His antagonist today could be his friend tomorrow, or vice versa. It was the way of politics. And it was exhausting.

She strolled in, fabulously accoutered as if on her way to a masquerade ball. He didn't judge. "Such a fine day for a visit," he told her as they each used both hands to shake warmly.

"How have you been?" she asked as the first move, pawn to king three, a conservative effort.

"Never better. And you?" He brought his knight out in a more aggressive counter-move, challenging her to one-up his claim of superior health.

"I am ready to travel," she replied. He raised one eyebrow, the subtlest of plays, which forced his opponent to take her piece back and move again. "Sagittarius Major."

He ushered her into her seat. She had brought out the queen early to lay waste across the board. Then again, maybe she was playing checkers.

"What do you wish to discuss, Secretary Anderson?" Binlow had tired of the game. He was now playing darts and had thrown his first at her face.

"The Green Door. We should have jurisdiction." Her claim had already been adjudicated in the UH, which spoke for all humanity. The archaeological find was on a planet situated conveniently at the other end of a wormhole. Close, timewise. Seventy-five light years away as the crow flew.

"You are a member of the UH and have your say in the matter, as every member has. The UH will retain jurisdiction. Humanity speaks with one voice. Is there anything else?" The cold of space could not have rivaled the tone of his voice.

"You don't understand what you have. You idiot!" Her face turned red with her instantaneous transition to fury. "It's an alien portal, technology that needs to be secured and brought back to Earth. We have scientists waiting to examine it, but who do you put in charge of it? A philosopher? You, sir, will be remembered for all time as the idiot who looked an alien in the face and refused to acknowledge his existence."

She glared as if the taunt were going to elicit a response. It did, but not what she was expecting.

He laughed softly as he contemplated the words. "Of course, aliens built it. But why?" He leaned toward her, holding his hands together as if praying. "The scientists will get their turn in due course. Whenever Somal decides to give them their turn."

She readied a retort, but it fizzled before delivery. Secretary Anderson settled for clamping her mouth shut and shaking her head.

Binlow stood. "One last thing. Please don't ever come to my office and call me names. Show yourself out."

As if by magic, the door opened, and his assistant Beatrice held it for the ambassador's imminent departure. He turned his back on the woman and returned to his seat, angling behind his computer screen so he didn't have to look at her.

What good was power if he couldn't wield it on occasion? She huffed on her way out.

Checkmate...

Now that you see how easy it is, start writing!

I hope you've enjoyed *Write & Sell Compelling Fiction*, hope you've gleaned at least one gem from it that will help your writing and hope to see your novels on the nation's bookstands alongside mine. If you want to see how these tips and techniques are applied, pick up one of my novels or if you are into science fiction, give one of Craig's a try.

Also writing as L. Jay Martin, Larry Jay Martin, Kathy Lawrence, and with Kat Martin, Bob Burton and Mike Bray. Craig writes as Craig Martelle, CH Gideon, and has a line of adventure mysteries under the name of Misti Forest.

L. J. Martin is the acclaimed, award-winning author of over forty novels and ten nonfiction books. He was raised in the deserts of California, wrangled and packed horses throughout the Sierra, and later rode and hunted Montana, where he now lives with his wife, NYT bestselling romantic suspense and historical romance author Kat Martin. L. J. was in real estate development for much of his life, selling over one hundred million dollars in transactions the last year he worked in the field. He's traveled the world over, and dealt with some of the most powerful companies in the country. He knows the boardrooms and backrooms of America, as well as her deep forests and wild high country. The Martins winter in California when not travelling for research on their novels.

The Zebra novels were published as L. Jay Martin; the Avon, co-written with wife Kat, as Kathy Lawrence; the Bantam novels and the Doubleday novel were all written as Larry Jay Martin. Subsequent novels, mostly from Pinnacle, were written as L. J. Martin and co-written with (and as) Bob Burton, and with Mike Bray. Most of my novels have been printed in Large Print and produced in audio, as well as ebooks. For more on Kat and me see:

www.katbooks.com

www.ljmartin.com

CRAIG MARTELLE'S OTHER BOOKS

Craig Martelle's other books (listed by series and here for convenience, but after the appendices you can find Craig's author notes and contact information)

Terry Henry Walton Chronicles (co-written with Michael Anderle) – a post-apocalyptic paranormal adventure
Gateway to the Universe (co-written with Justin Sloan & Michael Anderle) – this book transitions the characters from the Terry Henry Walton Chronicles to The Bad Company
The Bad Company (co-written with Michael Anderle) – a military science fiction space opera
Judge, Jury, & Executioner (also available in audio) – a space opera adventure legal thriller
Shadow Vanguard – a Tom Dublin series
Superdreadnought (co-written with Tim Marquitz)– an AI military space opera

Metal Legion (co-written with Caleb Wachter) (coming in audio) – a military space opera

The Free Trader – a young adult science fiction action adventure

Cygnus Space Opera (also available in audio) – A young adult space opera (set in the Free Trader universe)

Darklanding (co-written with Scott Moon) (also available in audio) – a space western

Mystically Engineered (co-written with Valerie Emerson) – Mystics, dragons, & spaceships

End Times Alaska (also available in audio) – a Permuted Press publication – a post-apocalyptic survivalist adventure

Nightwalker (a Frank Roderus series) with Craig Martelle – A post-apocalyptic western adventure

End Days (co-written with E.E. Isherwood) (coming in audio) – a post-apocalyptic adventure

Successful Indie Author – a non-fiction series to help self-published authors

Metamorphosis Alpha – stories from the world's first science fiction RPG

The Expanding Universe – science fiction anthologies

Monster Case Files (co-written with Kathryn Hearst) – A Warner twins mystery adventure

Rick Banik (also available in audio) – Spy & terrorism action adventure

Published exclusively by Craig Martelle, Inc

The Dragon's Call by Angelique Anderson & Craig A. Price, Jr. – an epic fantasy quest

APPENDIX A - RESEARCH BY LJ MARTIN

Write it right!

If you don't, you'll be called on the carpet by someone who knows it's wrong and western readers know the West. Historical readers, oftentimes, have an intimate knowledge about the time frame they like to read about. If your hero is a contemporary cop or FBI agent or microbiologist, there's an expert out there who'll call you on the carpet. Editors read thousands of well-written, well-researched novels, and they generally know one hell of a lot about the subject. If you write about the Roman Empire, believe me an expert in Roman times will be one of your readers. Be ready; be right.

If your hero pulls a Colt (yes, I know it should be Colt's) peacemaker in 1872, somebody is going to write you a letter and tell you it wasn't on the market until 1877. The reason it should be Colt's, by the way, is that advertisements of the time said Colt's, and consequently Colt firearms were referred to as Colt's, as in Colonel Colt's. However, if the hero pulls it on the first page of your novel and the editor is astute enough to know it wasn't yet on the market, then he'll begin to doubt all your facts, and your ability. And you won't sell your book.

One of the greatest liars of the twentieth century preached: Tell them three truths and they'll believe your next statement—even if it's a lie.

As a writer, tell them three truths and they'll accept the next fictional point as the truth. It's a form of suspension of disbelief. Involve the reader with accurate time and place, and the odds are much greater that the reader will become involved with your story.

If you don't know a lot about time and place, you can find out through research.

To me, research is a large part of the fun of writing. Reading everything—from other writers' western or historical novels, to dictionaries of old western terms, to journals and diaries—is enjoyable. In fact, at times, when I'm supposedly researching a specific item, I find myself reading away, lost in the enjoyment of the research material.

You want to research for accuracy of time and place, learn what a specific item is called—the leather strap that binds the cinch (girth in English riding) to the cinch ring on a Visalia saddle, for instance—but when you find the name of the latigo, you want to use it properly in the sentence. That will add credibility to your writing.

I remember a story from a *Murder She Wrote* teleplay that best exemplifies poor research. One of the characters was a rodeo clown, who had the job because he was too broken down physically to do anything else around the rodeo. Anyone who knows rodeo knows that the clown, or bullfighter, is probably the best athlete in the arena—probably in the state—probably one of the best in the world. He'd better be, because if he's not, he'll soon be hamburger. The whole time I watched that episode, I watched not to be entertained by the drama, but to be entertained by the writer's and producer's ineptness. I was laughing at them, not with them. And I'll bet that writer is now DDR, which is vernacular around my house for "down de road." Or he should be, but Hollywood perspicacity and veracity are among the last to be trusted.

Thank God most of their shows were set in Cabot Cove, where they know what they're doing and do it extremely well.

I don't know about you, but I'd hate to think a reader was reading my novels because he was entertained by the mistakes. Shudder!

In science fiction, physics is physics, even in the world of make believe. Take *Star Trek* for example. Acceleration to fantastic speeds would turn the crew into jelly, but they compensate for that with the inertial dampeners. There are no such things as we can't overcome inertia. Not yet anyway. Or create artificial gravity. We've all seen people floating in space. Throw in a science fiction scene where a spaceship loses artificial gravity and have people figure out how to move around while floating. The added realism of today, with the power of future science. Faster than light speeds, stable wormholes, move the plot along without too much handwavium. Craig added an ion drive in his Cygnus Space Opera series. That is technology of today. Any reader can look it up and see that Craig does it justice.

Tell three truths. Hook the reader with believability before stretching the fabric of reality.

WRITING FROM HISTORY:

Never, never, never should you lack for a story, a plot, characters, locations, etc., etc., because they are all there in histories, biographies, journals, newspapers, and other historical sources. Never should you lack for a plot in contemporaries, because there are millions in the newspapers, on the TV, and on the Internet, on a daily basis. You just have to tune in to them, and not with the remote.With your mind.

When I became interested in Edward Fitzgerald Beale, by reading a biography, I decided that he was the most unsung of western heroes.

Unlike John Charles Fremont, who had Jessie to chronicle his escapades, or Robert Field Stockton who kept a full-time biographer on staff to chronicle his, or Custer who had his wife, Libby, Beale did not seek or desire publicity. Yet the adventures and accomplishments that surrounded him eclipsed those of all other western heroes. I realize that's a large statement, and hope you'll read *Rush to Destiny* so I can help prove it to you.

Beale's life is recorded in three excellent biographies, as well as in the biographies and journals of his contemporaries, and in his own journal and letters.

When I sat down to write a novel based on this man's life, I was faced with a number of dilemmas. First, I knew I could not write about Beale without staying true to his life and adventures —and thank God, Beale's life needed no embellishment from a fiction writer. But what was the driving line of Beale's life, a driving line that would transfer to a novel and keep a reader interested? A driving line is something I always strive to *know* when I start a novel, for it's the road map I follow to a great extent. When I realized that I could not do Beale's life justice in one short (130,000 word) novel, I decided to write only the first half of his life and end the story with the successful taking of California, the fulfillment of Manifest Destiny, and Beale's completion of the survey for the first all-weather wagon road to the state. The unification, if you will, of the country, east and west, and the culmination of a dream.

With that in mind, I sat with thirteen tomes in a semicircle behind my desk chair. The three Beale biographies were most often reached for, but other biographies (Kit Carson's, Fremont's, etc.) were also in easy reach. I also had Bancroft's and other histories, including two Spanish translated histories. I wanted to tell the story of the California revolution from both sides.

Each time I would determine what scene fell next (a determination motivated by "keeping the story moving") I would reach for my resource material and read that particular segment, if covered, in each of those thirteen tomes. I did not try and read them in advance and take notes—although I did read them all in advance to get the flavor of the man and the time. Why not keep studious notes? Because I didn't know if I was going to use a particular scene or segment from his life, and it would have been time wasted. Be careful, in your writing, with 'over research.' Research is fun and interesting for me, and, at times, you'll find you'd rather be researching than writing. It's an easy trap to spring upon yourself.

I did learn that even distinguished historical scholars differ greatly in historical reporting. As a "for instance," I had about five different numbers for the deaths resulting from the Battle of San Pasqual. What good would it have done to keep conflicting notes? But I was not deterred. I determined what I thought was most accurate from the material at hand, and charged forward. History, as it's been often said, is most often written by the victors.

Never forget that your first responsibility as a writer of fiction is to entertain. I was not trying to write another biography of Beale; that had been done, and done well, three times. I decided I would be very happy if *Rush to Destiny* was read, if it entertained readers, and would be even more happy if they learned a little accurate history along the journey and came to respect the man. What better way to teach history than with the spice of adventure thrown in—and seldom are history tomes able to accomplish this effectively.

Consequently, if Beale's journals said, "Indians attacked, killed a mule," I wrote that as a three-page scene. Yes, I took artistic liberties. No, I had no way of knowing if the dialogue I wrote was accurate, or even close to what was actually said when those Indians attacked. I did know who was there (at least in the Beale camp) and that a mule was killed in an Indian attack—and that the incident and where it lay in the time line of Beale's life, and its location, was factual. Beale and his party, and some hungry or footsore Indians in search of a mule, provided me with a great scene in the middle of the Arizona desert.

One of the nicest compliments I've ever received as a writer was from a high school history teacher (the book was on the high school's reading list) when he said "My students learn more California history from your novel than from their texts, and love doing it." I still smile at the thought.

By the way, when writing about actual historical characters,

I never, NEVER, attribute deeds to them that are not related in some accurate, well documented, historical way. I recently read a historical novel that contained a scene in which one of the early California explorers was the attacker in an attempted rape. He was an *actual* character out of history. Unless I had evidence of this man being prosecuted and found guilty, I would never take such liberties with a man's memory. When we write fiction, there are too many characters who are available strictly out of our imagination. There's no reason to sully the reputation of an actual historical figure. How much easier and more appropriate would it have been for the writer to invent a character, rather than besmirch the name of a factual one.

The writer, even the fiction writer, is imbued with a trust. That trust should be to write accurately when dealing with factual characters. We all know that people tend to believe what they read, fact or fiction. Not to say that you can't let your muse run wild in any other situation, with any fictional characters, but when you've worked hard to develop a relationship with a reader—and he's in your imposed trance—don't take advantage of him by filling him with inaccuracies that confuse and mislead. There's a line between fiction and fact that shouldn't be crossed. Orson Welles discovered that when he first broadcast a fictional alien invasion, and found himself faced with a panicked country and a few suicides.

Use discretion lest your *fiction* be mistaken for *fact*. Even if this notion seems old-fashioned, it should never go out of vogue.

There is no tool more valuable for writing about history than the newspapers of the time. Obviously, if you're writing about the Roman Empire, you'll have a little trouble getting a copy of the local scandal sheet, but if you're writing about the late eighteenth or the nineteenthth century, great papers are available either for purchase (sources mentioned elsewhere in this book) or from your local library.

Newspapers tell you what was being used as medicine, what a meal cost at the local boarding house or hotel; where the boarding houses and hotels were in the town; the schedules of stages, steamships, and railroads, and where they were bound from or headed; what real estate was selling and renting for; what was happening with local politics, etc., etc., etc.

Newspapers give you the flavor of the time and place.

I never begin writing a piece set in the mid-to-late 1800s without picking up my copy of Alfred Doten's journals (University of Nevada Press), covering his life in Virginia City, Nevada, from 1849 to 1903. Doten was a newspaper journalist and kept a prolific diary—however, before he married he put an eraser to the more colorful passages. You can learn a lot about a person's day-to-day life from reading his journals.

Not only do newspapers and journals give you insight into time and place, but they give you plot material—maybe even whole plots. You can fictionalize from what you read as fact, and unless you're writing a biographical novel, change *everything*—the town, the characters, etc. That way you won't have to worry about distorting a piece of actual history.

To give you an example of writing from history and how closely I practice what I preach, here is a sample of the author's *Historical Notes and Acknowledgments,* which follow *Rush to Destiny*. A few footnotes will follow this sample (not included in the book, though I wish they had been) to offer additional explanation.

The author makes no claim to being a biographer, but has attempted to utilize history accurately in his writing, incorporating actual dispatches, letters, and newspaper accounts. Hopefully, this novelistic style offers accurate history, dates, and events in an entertaining form.

The author would like to express his admiration and appreciation to the following, whose fine nonfiction books were of immeasurable help:

Stephen Bonsal, *Edward Fitzgerald Beale: A Pioneer in the Path of Empire.*

Carl Briggs and Clyde Francis Trudell, *Quarterdeck and Saddlehorn: The Story of Edward F. Beale.*

Gerald Thompson, *Edward F. Beale & the American West.*

William A. DeGregorio, *The Complete Book of U.S. Presidents.*

And others too numerous to mention.

Almost all of *Rush to Destiny* is founded in fact, either gleaned from the biographies noted above, from the Beale Papers in the Beale Branch of the Kern County Library (named after Edward Fitzgerald Beale and located on Truxtun Avenue, which was named for his son), or from other related biographies or journals. The Beale Memorial Library has microfilm copies of those documents on file in the National Archives, where they require nine feet of shelf space. The general flow of events in the novel is very close to accurate, as are all dates. Ned Beale, as you have noted, was a very busy man. The author has used creative license to recreate actual conversations and to invent conversations to inform the reader or to fill in action. Where Beale's journal might note, "Indian attack, killed a mule," the author has expanded that into a whole scene. Even using this creative license, the author is sure, after intensive research, that Ned Beale's life was even more exciting than portrayed here.

Of interest, since they played such an important role in Beale's life, are some of the following: referred to lovingly as "her";

The Independence: Ned sailed on the third *Independence*, built in 1814, and razed from an eighty-four-gun frigate to a fifty-four-gun frigate in 1836. She was sold by the Navy in 1914. (1)

The *Congress*: Ned sailed on the fourth *Congress*, a frigate of forty-four guns. She was launched in 1841 and sunk by the Confederate ram *Virginia* on March 8, 1862. The wreck was later raised and sold.

The *Levant*: Luckily, Ned was not aboard the second-class sloop when she was lost in a storm with all hands in the Pacific in 1860.

The *Savannah*: A frigate of forty-four guns, Ned was aboard the second, built in 1820. She was sold by the Navy at the Norfolk Navy Yard in 1883.

The *Cyane*: Also a second-class sloop, of eighteen guns, she was built in 1837 and sold in California in 1887.

The *Constitution*: A forty-four-gun frigate, she was built in Boston in 1797. She is still afloat. (2)

The following notes or explanations are offered in chronological order, beginning with the Prologue:

Beale family memoirs relate young Ned's scrap in the Washington streets, its motivation, and the fact that Andrew Jackson broke it up. Later, Emily Beale took advantage of Jackson's reputed offer, and relied on his referral to get Ned his

Navy appointment. Jackson was called Andy-by-God as a result of his propensity to use the phrase.

When Ned entered the Navy, as a result of his father's death and family financial problems, he wore a coat on which his mother had sewn his grandfather's large, out-of-style buttons. Those buttons became the cause of a fistfight, as a result of which, it was said, Ned gained the additional respect of his peers. Still, Ned prudently acquired a more conventional coat shortly thereafter.

Norvell Johanson is a fictional character, a combination of several enemies, both in the Navy and in politics, whom Beale acquired during his lifetime.

It is not known exactly how much time Ned spent in England, nor exactly what he did there as he would never, during his long life, talk about his exact mission.

George Bancroft, the Secretary of the Navy, whom Ned reported to on his return from England, is the same Bancroft who wrote several definitive histories of the United States, which were referred to by the author. He is no relation (at least the author could not establish one) to Hubert Howe Bancroft who wrote the definitive several-volume history of California, another several-volume history of Mexico, and a ten-volume history of the United States—all of which were referred to many times in the past by this author for this work, and which will be referred to many times in the future for other historical works. Among other accomplishments, George Bancroft founded the U.S. Naval Academy at Annapolis, served as U.S. minister to Great Britain, and was minister to Prussia and Germany.

Ned's exploits while with the Brazilian Squadron were one of the wild times in the young man's life. He made many notes in his journals, giving rise to the fictionalization portrayed herein.

The slave Jourdan was actually purchased (and promptly set free) by Ned in New Orleans just before the camel trip, but in many instances prior to that, Ned had Mexican, Indian, or black traveling companions. Jourdan, for the sake of this novel, has become many of them combined. The real Jourdan remained a free man, staying with Ned Beale as a trusted friend and working as his body servant until Beale's death. (3)

The dispatch Ned carried from Bancroft to Commodore Stockton, when Ned rejoined the *Congress* at Callao, Peru, is verbatim. A great deal of controversy among historians over the years contemplates other possible unwritten orders. The author has taken liberties in assuming what those were.

The passage made by the *Congress* from Callao to the Sandwich Islands (Hawaii), under Ned's command as ship's master, set a new crossing record for sailing vessels.

Sam Brannan's ship, the chartered *Brooklyn*, was in harbor with the *Congress*, and Stockton did sell Brannan and his Mormons one hundred muskets and one hundred fifty Allan's six-barrel revolvers—the finest weapon of its time. Though inaccurate, it would faithfully fire six shots without reloading. Unfortunately, sometimes it would also jump-fire, and more than one cylinder would fire at a time. Later, Ned would come across Brannan many times in San Francisco, where the Mormon leader became active in the Vigilantes. The dispatches read by Sloat's fictional secretary, O'Connel, are practically verbatim, but annotated, as is the proclamation that was posted wherever the flag was raised. Daingerfield Fauntleroy was the name of the purser of the *Savannah* and was the officer Sloat ordered to establish communications among the northern Alta California communities. This is an instance where I'm sure the reader believed the author took great literary license—but the name is factual.

.....Continued.....

Notes for this volume:

(1) There are a number of wonderful books telling the history of every ship ever commissioned by the Navy. I found one in my local library.

(2) I should have gone on to explain that the *Constitution* is not only afloat, but beautifully restored, in Boston Harbor. You can visit her and enjoy living history exhibits while aboard.

(3) I found an actual note on the back of the receipt for Jourdan's purchase where Beale, in his own hand, noted that he'd purchased and set the slave Jourdan free.

I subject you to this "out of context" material for a purpose. As you read it, you can begin to see the amount of actual historical data, or writing from history, that I do (or did at least in this novel) when writing about an actual character or incident. Admittedly, *Rush to Destiny* is different from the norm. My westerns are not based (at least not the primary protagonist) upon a factual character, although many of them are laced with them, and with factual incidents.

I hope you'll pick up a copy of *Rush to Destiny*, and read it and the notes that follow. Only then can you appreciate the amount of influence history had on that novel. You can also appreciate how little plotting I had to do, for Beale's early life was the plot. You can also appreciate how little characterization I had to invent, for Beale's life was peppered with the greatest and most fascinating characters of the time.

In many ways, *Rush to Destiny* was the most simple novel I've written. In many other ways, it was the most difficult.

> **"You really have to invent a kind of music for a character. You've got to get the sound of their celebration. The writing should take on a sense of personage...."**
> **Robert Stone, Writer**

DICTIONARIES:

If you can write without a dictionary you're a better person than I. I use more than one. In fact, I use six when writing westerns or historicals.

The Random House Dictionary of the English Language is the one I've referred to so many times. It's wonderful for a western or historical writer for the primary reason that, for example, when you look up the word Kerosene (it was originally a trademark and therefore was capitalized), it defines the word then gives you one of these— [1852] —that tells you when the word was first used. Don't use kerosene before 1852 or some smart copy editor will strike it out and say "Use coal oil or whale oil, dummy." It has the other wonderful features other dictionaries have, too, but the date the word was first used is the one I treasure most.

Western Words, a Dictionary of the American West by

Ramon F. Adams is one I mentioned earlier, and is a wonderful addition to the western and historical writer's library. Example:

Broomtail: A range mare with a long bushy tail. Usually shortened to broomie.

My Random House dictionary does not define broomtail.

A Dictionary of the Old West by Peter Watts.

Also one mentioned earlier and a more scholarly edition than the above, but with less authentic color of the time. It has wonderful illustrations.

The fourth is an *1846 edition of Webster's* that I found at a Friends of the Library sale and cost me $5.00. It will tell you if a word was in use at that time. Remember, many words may not appear in the dictionary.

I also occasionally refer to the fifth: *The 1811 Dictionary of the Vulgar Tongue*

Believe me when I tell you that this little jewel has words and phrases you'll never find in another dictionary.

Words are, or should be, fascinating to the writer.

Including their origins.

Words like lariat, for example, were born of misconceptions. When the gringo cowhand heard the vaquero refer to his *la reata*, he thought he was saying *lariat* and a new word was born. As was lasso from *lazo* (Spanish for rope), and many, many more.

All words didn't, and don't, appear in the dictionary, because language is always growing and changing.

The sixth is relatively new, by a fine western writer, Win Blevins, and includes over 5,000 terms. It's a must for any historical writer.

The Dictionary of the American West
Facts On File, Inc.
460 Park Avenue South
New York, New York 10016-7382

Invest in yourself, and buy the above for your library.

In addition, as I've mentioned before, there are wonderful dictionaries on hundreds of subjects.

TECHNICAL BOOKS:

I mentioned that I have to research my English usage. The two volumes below are the bibles of writers and editors.

The Elements of Style by Strunk and White

A thin volume that every writer needs to read, then reread, then refer to.

And:

The Chicago Manual of Style

It is by the editorial staff of the University of Chicago Press. A manual used by many editors and copy editors in New York. If you want to know when to capitalize, or how to write faltering speech in dialogue, or a thousand other things, this is one authority in common use.

It is okay to break convention, but do it consistently and not in such a way that you'll lose the reader. For example, the Chicago Manual calls for a great deal more commas than are practical. Commas slow the sentence, break up the flow. Sometimes that's good, and other times, you'll jerk your reader out of a perfectly good sentence. Technical perfection does not exsit, but do what you do for a reason that makes sense. If you don't know what to do, then use a reference to find options.

MAGAZINES:

There are three magazines that every aspiring western, historical, or romance writer should read. The first is aimed at romance, but has a lot of market news and flows over into other genres. The next two are helpers in the process of writing and the market. The last is specific as to the business of writing and publishing.

The Writer's Digest

Online - https://www.writersdigest.com/

The Writer

Online - https://www.writermag.com/

Publisher's Weekly

Online - https://www.publishersweekly.com/

The first two magazines won't get you published, but they will tell you what other writers are thinking and doing, how to better your writing, and will keep you judging your own work and comparing it to others.

Publisher's Weekly is an industry magazine that talks about the publishing industry and book selling. At one hundred bucks plus per year, it's less important for a beginning writer than the other two, but well worth reading at the library as you wander through, doing research. It also has genre-targeted issues, and if you are interested, say, in children's books, then I would make sure to look up the couple of issues they do on that subject each year. Follow this publication for no other reason, than to study what writers and publishers are doing.

There are many genre specific magazines and newsletters. There's a newsletter specifically for medieval times, etc., etc. Dig in your library to find publications that are specific to the time and place you want to write about. For example, I'm working on a novel set around a United States Fish and Wildlife law enforcement officer, so I'm taking a Game Warden magazine. You learn not only about the job, but about the vernacular.

There are dozens of regional magazines which are excellent sources of material and excellent markets for regional writers.

And now the most important resource you have, a virtual world's largest library, is on your desk. The Internet. I keep a folder on my computer desktop simply titled "Links" and if and when you find an invaluable site on the Web, merely drag the link into that file. I probably have two dozen links there. And I add to them at least once a week. Why not list them here? As you can see, there's a variety of subjects. I've eliminated the personal ones, such as banking links:

Free SEO And Webmaster Tools
GoAnimate - GoAnimate Themes
Goodreads | Recent Updates
Google AdWords- Keyword Tool
Head shots - Tom Smarch Photography - Tom Smarch - Documentary,
HOT DAMN Designs!
imgur- the simple image sharer
Keyword Analysis Tool - Market Samurai
Khan Academy
Kindle Mojo! By Indie Authors for Indie Authors!

Link Generator, Create a Link With Text or an Image | MyspaceGen
Locating the Sweet Spot- What Will TV Channels Pay for Your Doc-
Mapping the 2010 U.S. Census - NYTimes.com
My Page - Number One Book Club
Sales Rank Tracking for Author Book Sales on Amazon | NovelRank
Sandvox Website creation for Mac that's as easy to use as the Mac
Shorten Links bitly | ♥ your bitmarks
State Facts | Bankrupting America
Turn your phone into the ultimate safety device | Life360°
Video Lessons & Resources
Worldometers - real time world statistics
www.vook.com-blog-wp-content-uploads-2011-10-ebookErrors2.pdf.Webloc

HOW TO WRITE:

In the final analysis, you have to write and write and write to learn how to write. But after you begin, these works will help you discover what you're doing wrong.

How to Write Western Novels by Matt Braun is a fine presentation by an accomplished writer. It is published by Writer's Digest.

The Western Writer's Handbook, edited by James L. Collins is a collection of articles by accomplished western writers and is well worth reading. It is published by Johnson Books, in Boulder, Colorado.

How to Write Best Selling Fiction by Dean R. Koontz is not specifically about writing westerns or historicals, but is a general how-to-write-well book. It is also published by Writer's Digest, but is out of print. I ran into Koontz at an American Booksellers Association convention and he told me he wished his "how to" book would go away, but it's still a fine work beginning writers can put to good use. It's hard to find, but worth it.

Make Every Word Count by Gary Provost is not specifically about writing westerns. Like the Koontz book, it is an excellent how-to-write book. It is published by Writer's Digest. Gary was a fine teacher and a great craftsman.

And there are literally hundreds, if not thousands, of others. Genre specific ones for the general genre in which you write and then basic craft and writing books by some of both big names and relative unknowns, like Stephen King's *On Writing*, John Truby's *The Anatomy of Story,* Randy Ingermanson's *How to Write a Dynamite Scene Using the Snowflake Method,* or Jessica Brody's *Save the Cat! Writes a Novel,* and so many more. But don't let yourself get quagmire in books about writing. The key to writing is writing.

Don't just read about writing. Practice writing. Every single day, write more words, different words. Craft the prose. Tighten the sentences. Trim the fat. Remove the redundancy. Write for character impact. Write for flow. Write to keep the readers reading and hungry for me, even after your book ends.

NEWSPAPER SOURCES:

I've mentioned several times that old newspapers are a great source of time and place information. If you're not fortunate enough to live near the town you're going to write about, and can't find the town newspaper from the time period you're writing about, find one from the time period. It will tell you what was going on nationally. But the local one is by far the best. It will tell you what was being smoked, drunk, used as liniment, what the price of a steak was at the local restaurant, what real estate sold for, what train and steamboat and stage schedules were, etc., etc. Great background.

Jim Lyons maintained a catalogue of old newspapers and resources. You can find some of his stuff here, http://jimlyons.com/siteindex.html, but it looks like old Jim has passed on. Again, your trusty friend, the internet, will be able to fill in the knowledge gap if you search diligently using the right keywords.

Jim is just one resource and I highlight him as an example.

THE LIBRARY:

Until you've really wandered through a good local library, you have no idea how much research material is available to you. Hidden in the bowels of most libraries are thousands of reference volumes that are not on the shelf. Many are not available to check out and can only be used on the premises.

Ask your librarian how to use the facility, or better yet, take a class. You will be amazed.

In specific areas, historical societies and museums may have libraries open to the public.

Many library collections of older works are now available online. Let Google flow and you'll be amazed at what you find, but you also have to be wary. Many internet sites purport to have expertise when they do not. Redundant information from independent sources will tell you whether you are on the right path or not.

***OTHER RESOURCES*:**

Can't afford to go to New York city to check out a location? Google Earth is the writer's BEST FRIEND. You've got to see it to believe it! I'm just beginning to discover the tremendous material available from the State and National Government. You can obtain ship passenger lists from the middle of the nineteenth century and immigration documents from that time. The National Archives is the scrapbook of the nation. Addresses of various local and national branches are available at the library. This saved me a trip to Las Vegas, all coming form Google Earth, in ten minutes:

From my crime novel *The Repairman*:

The Department of Public Safety State Fire Marshal's resides in a state office building on the southeast corner of E. Bonanza Road and North Veteran's Memorial Drive, north of the strip but pretty centrally located, just north of old Vegas. The modern building enjoys a glass curtain wall near the entrance. A fairly massive four-story concrete structure behind contains offices of the fire marshal and other state organizations such as Parole and Probation, with the convenience of a two-story parking garage to its west. Beyond the garage is a six-bay City of Las Vegas fire station. Behind it is additional parking, but a conventional street level lot.

To the south of both facilities is the Las Vegas Municipal

Pool, with lots of public parking. That's where I land the Harley, only a couple of hundred yards from the front entrance of the building housing the marshal's office, yet out of its sight. And there's a freeway onramp only a block farther on, and Freeway 93 has lots of open space, and lots of ramps to dump off onto other surface streets.

POSTAL HISTORY:

I happen to collect California express company covers—the envelopes carried on the stage coaches during the nineteenth century. In trying to determine the age of these collectibles, I've found books compiled by other philatelists which give the opening and sometimes the closing dates of town post offices. Among other things, you can find information on ghost towns and can determine if a town was in existence (at least if it had a post office) with postal history books.

I've also acquired excellent histories of Wells Fargo and Co. and the Butterfield Overland mail in my postal history wanderings. All of it is helpful in writing westerns and historicals, and most of it is available at the local library.

ON LINE SERVICES:

As I've mentioned before, and as most of you know, many excellent online services are available to the accomplished computer user. I use Google and Yahoo daily, or probably more accurately, hourly. Learn how to use them. The Internet has blossomed into an incredible source for research.

MISCELLANEOUS:

I will only list the few reference works I reach for with regularity to show you an example of the resources a western author has at his fingertips.

The 1811 Dictionary of the Vulgar Tongue
Bibliophile Books
https://www.amazon.com/Dictionary-Vulgar-Tongue-Francis-Grose-ebook/dp/B0082RKL16

A Timetable of Inventions and Discoveries
By Kevin Desmond
M. Evans & Company, Inc.
https://www.amazon.com/Timetable-Inventions-Discoveries-Pre-History-Present/dp/B001JTMR2U

The Timetables of History
Edited by Lawrence Urdang
Simon & Schuster, Inc.
https://www.amazon.com/Timetables-History-Horizontal-Linkage-People/dp/0743270037

Firearms of the American West
by Garavaglia and Worman
University of New Mexico
https://www.amazon.com/Firearms-American-1803-1865-Louis-Garavaglia/dp/0826307205 (1803-1865)
https://www.amazon.com/Firearms-American-1866-1894-Louis-Garavaglia/dp/0826307922 (1866-1894)

Costumes Through the Ages
https://www.amazon.com/Costume-Through-Ages-Illustrations-Costumes-ebook/dp/B00A73IZU2

There are hundreds of other local volumes on every subject of the old West and writing imaginable. And even more on crime. Kat must have a dozen books on fashions of the past.

The above are on your library shelves.

Your local bookstore will normally oblige you by ordering them if you don't want to write for them directly, and of course, the Web is eager and waiting.

Don't be bashful about searching the used bookstores, yard sales, etc., for resource books. I've found many there that were not on the library shelves and were out of print when I attempted to get them from the publisher.

DEALERS:

There are hundreds of dealers who specialize in western Americana, and in almost any subject you care to write about. And don't overlook the university presses.

How much are you willing to spend on your research or your craft? This is a tough question. People have spent vast sums and were no better for it. Others have spent nothing and learned nothing, while others learned a great deal at no cost. Your diligence is what will make the difference. As with most endeavors, if you are serious about a career as a writer, then don't short-change yourself. It will be what you put into it, and I'm not talking money. Maybe you want that expensive artifact as a motivator to keep writing your historical fiction. If that's what it takes, do what is right for you.

Craig writes science fiction. He does not have any items or special dictionaries on his shelves to help him. The internet is where he finds everything he needs to add and build realism on a fantastic backdrop.

BLOGS AND NEWS LETTERS:

I must admit that I'm not much of a newsletter subscriber; nor am I active enough in the blogging world. However, both are great resources, and the enterprising researcher should take advantage of them.

> **"Literature is of greater philosophical importance than history; whereas history reports things as they are, literature presents things as they might be, and ought to be."**
>
> **Aristotle**

APPENDIX B - SELLING TO LEGACY PUBLISHERS BY LJ MARTIN

Since the following was originally written, I've sold the large majority of my interest in Wolfpack Publishing, but Mike Bray continues on with great success. I just checked Amazon's Classic Western bestseller list and find twenty-seven of the top 100 titles (including my most recent *SHADOWS OF NEMESIS* at No. 2) published by Wolfpack Publishing. A recent study by a U.K. research firm listed Wolfpack Publishing as the U.S.A.'s number four in western publishing.

Now, the backstory:

For the first time in the thirty years I've been in publishing, authors have the opportunity to have their work seen, and hopefully purchased, by buyers all over the world. And that opportunity comes without the filter of some publishing house in New York City. It comes thanks to the Web and companies such as Amazon, Apple, Barnes & Noble, Kobo, Smashwords, and many others.

Is this good?

You bet it's good for the author who's willing to learn to write well, to write compelling fiction, to get it properly formatted, to design or have designed a cover that will attract buyers, and then to either work hard on the Web or hire or contract with others to do so. Craig has a book on that specific process – check out his How to Become a Successful Indie Author, book one of the Successful Indie Author series of non-fiction titles.

Is an easily accessible marketplace bad?

Yes and no. As of this writing, Amazon reports that it is adding thousands of new titles every day. That's a lot of competition.

I personally think the Web's the best thing to happen to authors since the invention of Guttenberg's printing press.

As a former mid-list writer who primarily wrote westerns, I was at the mercy of New York publishers who had twenty story buildings to pay for. They HAD to and HAVE to print books that will help pay those costs and they consequently assign huge overhead costs to every book they take on. But those of us who work out of our houses can look at a book differently, and our costs are infinitesimal as compared to those of Random House and others. They also had a front line of twenty-five-year-old Brown graduates who'd never been west of the Hudson—but that's another story altogether.

As a publisher of ebooks, I relish the opportunity to publish authors' backlists, books that have lain on shelves gathering dust, and am sending fat checks monthly to authors who'd given up on ever seeing another dime from books they'd written twenty-five years ago. And I love it. And I'm happy to report they love it as well.

We at Wolfpack Publishing are the guerrillas of publishing,

the fast free-moving force that is cutting a wide swath in the publishing world by getting product to the market quickly and by understanding this ever-moving target of book sales. We've brought 250 books to the market in the past fifteen months, and I don't mind saying that's a hell of an accomplishment. Not one dime was asked of authors in that process. We've constantly had a presence of from five to nine of the top twenty books on Amazon's classic western bestseller lists, and many on other lists as well. We love those backlists and what's more we love those books that well-established authors have submitted to their conventional publishing houses and have been told "Susan, you're a romance author with an established audience. Why rock the boat with this mystery?" Or they're told "Our sales force says this book falls through the cracks. Put it on the shelf. Write it off as good experience."

The hell with that.

Let's make some money with it. That's what Wolfpack Publishing does. We don't take on many single titles as we sell one book off another. Having lots of books by a single author in front of a buyer is our mantra. And that's done very well on the Web.

One of the GREAT advantages of the Web is the fact an author, particularly a mid-list author, would have been thrilled to see all six of his/her titles on a Barnes and Noble shelf at the same time. Odds are all they'd see is the last book. Now you go to the author's page on Amazon, or search for that author's title, and voila, you see every book that author's ever published, all before your eyes and probably all for sale to provide instant gratification to a hungry reader.

It's a boon to authors.

Is it bad?

Yeah, it has its drawbacks. You're now out there kicking, elbowing and scratching, competing with a million or more books. You've got to know what you're doing to rise anywhere near the top of this now huge marketplace.

Today, as I write this, my latest is No. 5 on Amazon's men's adventure list, No. 7 on the crime list, and No. 7 on their hard-boiled list. My last four have risen to No. 1 on those lists and I have every expectation this one will as well. This is thanks to the expertise of an associate who's a Search Engine Optimization (SEO) expert and knows how to sell on the Web. But they won't keep selling (and they have) unless they are compelling reads. Neither will yours.

Craig has been a top 100 science fiction on Amazon since March 6th, 2017. That's right, two and a half years as of this writing without a single day outside the top 100. How did he accomplish that? Books in series that compelled readers to keep reading. If they hadn't done that, he would not be a perennial fixture at the top of his trade.

I've got to take a moment to talk about Amazon and their phenomenal growth to the world's No. 1 bookseller and all the bitching and moaning coming from legacy publishers and booksellers all over the world.

I'm the original free enterprise guy.

I've had several careers over my seventy-seven years and am currently working on another one. I absolutely believe in the free enterprise system that's brought the world's greatest standard of living to those of us fortunate enough to be citizens of the United States of America. I've never spent five seconds complaining about another's success, and neither should you, nor should the legacy publishers. Get off your butts and compete, or grab a fishing pole and go to the lake and get the hell out of the way of those who are willing to work for it.

Yes, Amazon has the lion's share of the market. Why? Because they've earned it, that's why. But they can't do it without authors. And I believe they're smart enough to know that and will continue to treat authors very, very well. I personally get a check every month, as does Wolfpack Publishing. And we pay our authors monthly, within ten days of receiving the money. When I sell a book for $2.99 on Amazon, I make two bucks. And I get paid two months from the month of sales. When I was with legacy publishers, I would have to sell a book for $16.00 to make two bucks, and wouldn't see that money for two years and not then had they not been paid back for my modest advance.

I LOVE Amazon, and by extension, I love Barnes & Noble and Smashwords (which markets via Apple and others).

It's my belief that Apple will become the next major player in the book market. After all, they have more money in the bank than the United States of America, and handle it way, way better. I love Apple, as well as the fact they've made my writing and filmmaking life much easier. Will they ever overtake Amazon? I doubt it. And to be truthful as a free enterprise guy, I hope not, as Amazon has taken huge risks and established a market that didn't formerly exist. God bless them.

Let others whine. Learn how to work with the distributors while others work against them and you'll profit handsomely.

REJECTION:

The number one thing to remember about selling your novel is that you're bound to encounter rejection. *Jonathan Livingston Seagull*, the all-time, number-one most-translated novel, was rejected twenty-eight times!

It's part of the business.

Sometimes a rejection can be helpful—if it's not a form rejection. Some editors, particularly if you've submitted through an agent, will tell you in their rejection letter why the novel was rejected. It's much less painful to get an "all our slots are full through 1995," than "dull and plodding."

But if you get a "dull and plodding," reread your work and see if you think it can be improved. That's not to say you should accept all criticism from editors as commandments chiseled in stone. Even editors have bad days. If the editor who wrote "dull and plodding" had forgotten something on his way to work and returned to his apartment to find the Lower East Side Motorcycle Club lined up outside his back door accepting his wife's carnal hospitality, even a scathing remark about your masterpiece might be considered a compliment in his state of mind.

Every time I get a rejection, I figure something dire must have happened to the poor soul.

Don't try to second guess editors, don't take their comments as gospel, but learn from every rejection.

This also goes for bad reviews on your books. If you skipped past the gatekeepers and self-published, then your first feedback from a disinterested third party may be those reviews. If you get nine good ones and one bad review, the bad one may have been from someone having a bad day or possibly even someone who picked up your book by mistake. There also may be some gems that you can fix. Enter the power of the digital world. If there is an honest mistake, you can fix it and upload a new copy. Anyone who buys your book from that point forward will get the updated copy.

Some people won't read their reviews because they find them soul-crushing. Others won't read reviews because they don't trust the feedback. Take them all with a grain of salt, but don't miss the opportunity to learn how the readers perceive your story.

AGENTS:

A literary agent knows something that you, as a beginning novelist, don't—the publishing business.

They know who's looking for what. They know where to present your work and which editor at that company will be most inclined to like your particular style or subject matter.

They know contracts and how to protect your interests. If you don't have an agent, then at least find an intellectual property (IP) lawyer who will be able to protect your interests from the likes of big publishing and Hollywood. If you have the right story at the right time, people will not hesitate to make their fortunes off you. Make sure your interests are protected and that you get to make a fortune, too.

If you can get an agent, then trust him or her. Don't bet your writing life on them but give them a chance to perform for you. If they do, stick with them. They don't make money unless *you* do. They don't make more money unless you make more money. They'll push to bring your career along. Believe me, they want you to be a writing star almost as much as you want to be a star.

Unfortunately, getting an agent can be more difficult than

getting published. In fact, many writers don't get an agent until after they've sold their first or second novels. A legitimate literary agent doesn't charge you up front to read your work or represent you. They only make a commission if they sell your work—usually 10 to 15 percent of both the advance and the ongoing royalties. Consequently, they want work that will sell. And they usually get more for your work than you could, thus earning back the commission and really costing you nothing.

And the single most important reason to get an agent—your work will get read by editors if you're trying to go the traditional publishing route. Craig has never had an agent, as an alternative even though he has four books with a traditional publisher. He prefers self-publishing because of the control he exercises over his work and the reward in getting the full royalties. He does not have to split the profit with anyone.

Every publisher who accepts unsolicited manuscripts—some companies won't even open the package if it's not from an agent—has a "slush pile." A manuscript may linger in a slush pile for months and months before being picked up and glanced at by an editor. My first novel gathered dust in a slush pile for a year before an editor had an extra minute and happened to grab it. And buy it. If the work comes from an agent, it gets read without being chucked into the giant conglomeration of lonely works and writers' hopes—the slush pile.

You see, the editors want to maintain a relationship with agents, as agents provide them with publishable works—and do some of the preliminary work for them.

Submit your work to agents if you want to go that route. You can find a list of them online from more than one source.

Whether you submit to agents or directly to publishers,

remember these four letters—*SASE*. Self-Addressed Stamped Envelope. Enclose one of adequate size so they can mail your manuscript back to you without cost to them. Make *sure* it has adequate postage (and don't send postage from a meter unless you leave it undated). A better method is to enclose a stamped, self-addressed envelope. The way to get an agent or editor to read your work with a good frame of mind is to let them know you're professional enough to send a SASE.

All the above is applicable to submitting for legacy or brick and mortar publishers. More and more, in fact most, publishers are accepting digital manuscripts. Those great rooms full of ignored submissions are disappearing from publishers offices. And thank God for it. Who needs reams of paper now that we have hyperspace? But you must check and see if your manuscript will be welcome, and one way to do that is to attend conferences and meet with editors.

Don't use an agent who wants to charge you a reading fee.

But my favorite story regarding agents comes from Clive Cussler. Frustrated with not attracting an agent to his work, Cussler took the creative approach. He printed stationery as "Charles Winthrop Agency" and wrote leading agent Peter Lampack, who was at the William Morris Agency at the time, saying he primarily handled motion picture scripts and asking if Lampack would look at Cussler's work. He did, out of professional courtesy, and thinking he had met "Winthrop" somewhere. The rest is history. Even then it took Lampack five years or more to sell Cussler's then unusual work.

You may or may not want to be as creative as Mr. Cussler.

Look for lists of agents in The Writers Market and Literary Market Place in your local library.

SELF SUBMISSIONS TO PUBLISHING HOUSES:

All the below is applicable only to paper manuscript submissions. Most editors now want digital submissions, but find a way to get them to ask for same. The query letter is one way to accomplish this.

If you decide to submit yourself, write the best letter possible—a letter that opens with a hook or at least a strong statement. Tell them briefly what your book is about and why it is suitable for their line—and you'd better be sure it is. How? Read the kind of westerns, historicals, or novels in your area of interest and see which company publishes them.

Edit that letter carefully—it's your first exposure to an editor, telling him that you're a writer. List any writing credits you may have—local magazines, newspapers, etc. **Keep it short**—one page or less. Editors are busy.

If you don't submit digitally, then submit your manuscript on 8 1/2 x 11 inch 20 lb. white, each page with 25 lines of type, each with 60 characters maximum, making a 250 word page. Number each page (upper right hand corner, if possible) and put your name and the novel title in a header on each page. Use a clear (courier, if possible) type face, 12 point.

Try to find out the proper editor to whom to submit your novel. A company may have fifty editors and your sci-fi work may not be appreciated by the one who specializes in lesbian love stories—unless you're writing them.

If you write a query letter without sending the manuscript and they respond by saying they'd like to see three chapters and an outline, make sure you address it to that editor by name and put **MANUSCRIPT REQUESTED** on the cover of the package. It will zoom through the mail room directly to the editor's desk. Don't wrap it like it contained the Holy Grail; it's a sure giveaway that you're a beginning writer and an irritation to the editor who has to open it. A simple envelope will do.

Do not send your original!

Manuscripts have been lost by the most careful publishers, and another irate writer screaming over the telephone will only drive that publisher one step closer to becoming another of those who only accept agented manuscripts.

Be humble, be gracious, be wolverine tenacious.

A list of publishers and sometimes editors can be found in both the Writer's Market and Literary Market Place.

These people make the decisions about buying novels.

Study the racks to determine which publishers publish what you're writing, then call those publishing houses to find out what editors are buying what you have to sell.

And remember: SASE!

It doesn't hurt to check to make sure the editor is still at a particular company, or that the company is in the market for your particular genre at the moment you decide to submit.

Genre-specific magazines and genre-aligned craft groups within social media will give you a lot of information on markets.

And prepare yourself for the long game. If you self-publish, then your book could be putting money in your pocket while

I hope this book has helped you. I hope you'll be looking forward to reading yours and hope you'll read mine.

Good Luck with your novel!

THOUGHTS ON WESTERNS

So many poorly represented westerns have appeared on television and movies that it has almost destroyed the genre. Then along comes a good one and perception changes. Today's contemporary producers and directors continue to try to place twentieth century values, mores, and lifestyles in the nineteenth century. They portray children as assertive and mouthy when, in that era, "a child should be seen and not heard." They try to put women in business at a time when it was commonly believed that "a woman's place is in the home." There were exceptions, of course. They continue to write men who swear and wear their hats indoors in the presence of women, or at the table, when a man would have been horsewhipped for swearing in front of a woman and the nearest man would have at least reminded him to remove his hat, probably asking him, "Is your head cold?" Deadwood, the TV show, was dead wrong, but they played to a contemporary audience who cared little for history. Don't write away from all of the things that attract viewers to westerns and historicals. But that's not to say you can't write a great and historically accurate novel featuring a woman who rose to the top of most any profession in the nineteenth century —you can, and you can be historically correct, as long as you respect the little things, and as long as you write her as an anomaly, outside the norm.

Western and historical readers and viewers know the West and know history. They not only read western and historical fiction, but many read and study history—including journals and autobiographies. They know how it was in the West, or wherever and whenever they care to study.

Writers of both novels and film would do well to emulate them. Study time and place and write to it, not away from it.

But the western and historical genres are also changing for the better. Women are being written about accurately as strong, proud, women—as strong and sometimes stronger than the men of the time—who deserve to be admired and copied for the values they portray. The Native American is coming into his own, accurately chronicled as a proud people with values and mores that deserve being written from a Native American point of view.

And other minorities are finally being represented in westerns and historicals. Accurate writers are discovering that around most any 1870s southwest cattle drive campfire there would seldom be ten whites, but rather two blacks, six Hispanics, a Chinese cook and one white—or European, as whites were known in most of the Americas, and as they are still known to a good part of the world.

In a *Publisher's Weekly* article *Blazing a New Trail,* Dennis E. Showalter maintains that "American West themes are making a major comeback. The box-office success of Clint Eastwood's *Unforgiven* has made the western a hot Hollywood item." And more recently, shows such as *Hell On Wheels* have portrayed the West in a legitimate light.

The same can be said of most genres...they come and go. Today it's vampires, tomorrow God only knows.

Even though I will tell you what I feel is the easiest way to get published, and how to "write to" what New York views as the West, there are still great inroads to be made by writing away from these guidelines—but the risk of not getting your work sold is greater. But never write away from good time and place. It's not good writing to do so, and it's not good for the profession—unless you're writing a parody, such as *Blazing*

Saddles. And now, no matter what you write, you can self publish and possibly start a whole new genre. Hell, write what's in your heart and head and, if it's a great story, it'll find a home and maybe great success.

And that rule (like most of what I tell you) is made to be broken. The fact is, there are few hard facts in writing.

Romance represents 60 percent (or more) of the mass market paperback industry. A huge number. Women read 80 percent of all the fiction written in America and buy romance in huge quantities. Romance dominates ebook sales and the largest selling book of the last few years was the ultra sexy, ultra erotic, *Fifty Shades of Gray.* It started a gold rush to soft porn.

If you can write what makes them laugh, makes them cry, and turns them on, you can have a piece of this huge worldwide book market and see your romance novel alongside Kat's and those of many other fine writers on the nation's bookracks or online.

L'Amour didn't get his first novel published until he was forty-six. Mine came at forty-seven. Yours may come at seventeen or eighty-seven.

The first criteria for a novelist, as far as I'm concerned, is loving to read. If you enjoy reading mystery, romance, horror, fantasy, science fiction, westerns, or any other genre, then I suggest you turn your writing talents to the particular genre you love to read. You already know a lot about it—length, structure, basic rules such as a happy ending for a romance. A great, probably worldwide threat, for a thriller. You may not realize you know those things, but you do. And that's one of the reasons you should write what you love to read.

If you love to read novels, chances are you'll love writing them even more.

How else could you sit back, God-like, and become a cavalry general attacking the Cheyenne or a gunslinger walking down the main street of 1880 Dodge City or Tombstone to draw down on the fastest gun in the West? How else can you become a swashbuckling pirate or his petulant captured flame-haired heroine?

And if you don't like the way the action comes down, you can do it again. Writing is a wonderful way to make all those fantastic dreams you had as a youth, or have today, come true—moving from the pictures in your mind, through your keyboard, and onto the screen or at least on paper.

Dream, and get paid for it.

I've never been one for long, intricate, manuals that tell you every detail necessary to accomplish a goal—although this one continues to grow. I'm impatient. This book is designed to give you the hard-hitting facts about what and how. (The when, why, and where is up to you.)

I will also give you some insight into reference materials and books. After a number of years of collecting, I have most of these mentioned in my own personal library, but all of them, and many more, may be found in local lending libraries, or may be interbranched or intercity borrowed and, of course, the world's largest library and resource is in front of you—your computer and the Internet.

The Web is now the ultimate research tool; no one could have a reference library to match it. But you have to be careful. Not all the information you might find on the Web is accurate. Anyone can post.

I've also included a list of weekly, monthly, and bi-monthly magazines that will help you with craft and keep you up on the marketplace. These, too, are available at the library; although some may be out of print by the time you read this. The market changes; magazines come and go.

You'll also share with me the agony of defeat. In writing, it's called a rejection slip. In today's self publishing world, it's called "no check in the mailbox." But sometimes you can use even rejection slips to your benefit! So if your writing glass is half empty, a rejection slip is defeat; if it's half full, it's a learning process. (Of course, most writers believe the place for rejection ships is next to the toilet for a more practical use.) No sales of your book should tell you something as well—probably it's "go back to the learning process." Sometimes it's merely go back to learning how to sell on the Web.

With the exception of a couple of optioned screenplays, every dime Craig and I have made writing has been made from westerns, historical romances, historicals, science fiction, mysteries, suspense, or thrillers (and a few bucks from articles and nonfiction), so the meat of this book is going to center on writing well, not writing in any particular genre because we've written to many of them.

The acquisition editor's first obligation to the publishing house is to stock the shelves with the standard product—the proven sellers. Only one in every hundred books they edit will they reach out. And remember, they've probably read, or partially read, five thousand or more manuscripts to get those hundred they bought. The reality is that a million manuscripts a year get submitted and 3,500 are published in mass-market fiction, numbers that are constantly changing. The odds against a truly unusual book getting to the market are huge. But when they do, they are sometimes the huge sellers. Take *Fifty Shades of Grey* as an example. Or don't.

Jonathan Livingston Seagull, among the all-time best-selling novels and the most translated novel, bar none, from the English language (at least when I wrote this; I'm sure this has changed), was turned down twenty-eight times before it found a home. It was a short, unusual story. Now it's a short, unusual story translated into more languages than any other novel ever published.

But if you want to get comfortably published, don't try to reinvent the wheel. Write to the market. Make it easy on the editors. Give them a product they're used to, one they can get on the shelf with little effort on their part or that of the copy editor. One that the publishing house knows how to sell, sells, and makes money. If you want to self publish, write anything you want. Just don't be disappointed when it's hard to market. That said, take Ray Bradbury's advice.

I once spoke at a college seminar on writing where the renowned science fiction writer Ray Bradbury was the featured speaker. After my small portion of the seminar, I attended Ray's keynote address—and found myself being berated for giving the exact advice above: "Write to the market," although it had been related to him in a different manner than I'd represented. "I also said, write from the heart." And "money isn't everything."

Bradbury, who sold his first brilliant novel, *Fahrenheit 451*, at the ripe old age of twenty-one or so, believed that all writers should be like him—brilliant—and merely write a brilliant novel and go on to fame and fortune. Thank you, Ray. But some of us have to grind it out the hard way, and would like to make a little money, and get a few pats on the head, along the path. Now that you're gone, I truly hope you've found a place in heaven—with a word processor close at hand. Craig is known as the blue-collar author. A Marine and lawyer by trade, but success was hard earned, publishing his first book at the age of fifty-four. There are far more examples of authors toiling at the word mines, getting better with each new book, than there are of those whose first book is a runaway hit.

Yes, if possible, write a brilliant, unorthodox novel and get rich and famous. But the odds are you'll languish and slip away from writing when you find a pile of rejection slips building window-sill high beside your desk (or toilet), unless you're wolverine tough. Or when you visit the mailbox, time and time again, and find that Amazon has forgotten to send you a check. And Amazon doesn't forget. You forgot to sell your book. Many who might evolve into brilliant productive writers will go by the wayside if expecting, and being disappointed by, the lack of fame and fortune from a first novel or from not selling a first, or second, or third novel. Many productive and successful writers did not sell a manuscript until they had written a half-dozen novels. I remember a story about Danielle Steel. It was reported that she sold her first novel, only to receive rejections on her next five. That would be even tougher in many ways than not selling your first.

Editors look forward to receiving their paychecks regularly. If they don't stock the shelves with books that sell, paychecks stop coming, and they are looking for another job. They look for product to fill the slots they have open—tried and true genre product that fits the slot. And you'll be unusual if you continue to write and self publish when you get no checks in the mailbox.

AUTHOR NOTES

I am a blue-collar author. I have a law degree, but that doesn't matter, not when it comes to writing. What matters is the willingness to work hard at this thing called self-publishing. I've worked harder, not smarter, on a number of things. I've been fairly successful, but I have so much more to learn.

I mention 20Booksto50k® a few times in this book. This is a premise that Michael Anderle came up with based on the sales he saw from his first four books. If he wanted to retire to Cabo San Lucas, he figured he would be able to live comfortably on $50k per year. If he had twenty books that earned $7.50 per day for all, he would have a comfortable life. It's not twenty books in a year. It is simply twenty books making a minimum daily amount. The power of backlist, the power of releases, and a growing readership showed that the numbers could be orders of magnitude higher.

We have a Facebook group with that name. 20Booksto50k® is the DARPA of indie publishing. It is the ultimate research and development center where we try different things. Where we have a vast smorgasbord of options from which we can pick and choose what we want to try. And we have a great number of success stories, too. Hope is the greatest condiment you can sprinkle on your efforts. Work hard at the right things.

I've published over four million words by the time Mike Bray asked me about partnering with Larry on this book, even though the book had already been in publication for over ten years. But ten years is forever in this industry. Larry had the core of this book locked up tightly. We put the traditional publishing slant in the appendices and kept the focus on managing your manuscript yourself. Writing the words, and rewriting them until you had something that resonated.

With the readers, because they are the ones betting on you. It takes a great story written in a compelling way. We all have that great story within, but can we put it onto paper? I hope this book helps with that. A lot of food for thought and as you write, you may want to refer back to the examples and see how you're doing with your own work.

Self-publishing is a calling. We see all kinds of articles on how little authors make, and that most don't have more than a book or two published. Who wants to be mediocre at something that is in your soul? Stand out from the crowd and take this business seriously. You can create great art, but don't sit back and lament that it doesn't sell. That's on you, and you can do it. If you want to pay someone else ninety cents on the dollar to publish your stuff for you, you can do that, but then you'll lament how the middleman is taking all your money. Don't!

Self-publishing is the way to go to maximize the profitability of your art. Who doesn't want seventy-percent royalties? If you don't want money for your art, you can do that, too, but then you don't need to be reading these books. My books are about helping your personal financial situation by doing what is possible with your books.

Embrace the beauty of life! I live 150 miles from the Arctic Circle. I'm writing this in August of 2019 and it is raining a fair bit, as happens in August and the fall nip is in the air. August is when it turns cold this far north. September is fall and then winter starts in October into April. Spring until the middle of May when summer starts for its short visit.

Shout out to the review crew! What a great bunch of people. I'm sure I left someone off. No slight intended, just an aged mind and busy soul who failed to annotate who got back to me.

- Robert Tillisley
- Lasairiona McMaster
- James Caplan
- Ashli Faron
- Kim Dorothy
- Troy A. Hill
- Lyn Worthen

Thank you all. You helped make this book better and more

helpful through your valuable input. We rewrote this book a solid three times to make sure of the flow and information. We removed a bunch of words and added even more.

This isn't a book about advertising. That stuff is hard! Publishing? Well, that's hard, too, but a different kind of hard. Writing is the hardest as it's an individual journey. Writing the book gets easier the more you do it. Some people say that only the first million words are hard. I'll tell you that the words can be hard or easy. It depends on the story. And they do get easier the more you write. With anything, practice can make the difference. Work hard at the right things and one day, you'll find that you are an author and have been all along.

Learn what you need to know when you need to know it and you won't be overwhelmed. No one knows it all, and just when you think you've become an expert, something changes, and we all get to start afresh.

But that's the great thing about being an indie—a self-published author. We flex and get moving once again.

There's nothing like it. You are responsible for your own success, which is the greatest feeling in the world.

Peace, fellow humans

Craig Martelle

If you liked this book, please give it a little love and leave a review. I'm not big on non-fiction. My wheelhouse is science fiction! So, you don't need to join my newsletter since I'm not going to promote non-fiction there. But if you like science fiction...

You can join my mailing list by dropping by my website www.craigmartelle.com, or if you have any comments, shoot me a note at craig@craigmartelle.com. I am always happy to hear from people who've read my work. I try to answer every email I receive.

You can also follow me on the various social media pages that I frequent.

Amazon—www.amazon.com/author/craigmartelle

Facebook—www.faceBook.com/authorcraigmartelle

My web page—www.craigmartelle.com

Printed in Great Britain
by Amazon